TULE REVIEW
2023

Tule Review, founded in 1993, is published by The Sacramento Poetry Center, a not-for-profit, tax-exempt organization registered in the State of California, and funded through our memberships, public donations, and the Sacramento Office of Arts and Culture. Contributions to SPC are appreciated and tax-deductible.

The Sacramento Poetry Center
1719 25th Street
Sacramento, California 95816
sacpoetrycenter.org

TULE REVIEW 2023
© 2023
ISBN 9798852044655

Authors and artists maintain copyright of their work.

Cover art: "Sacramento Springs to Life at Oakmont" © 2023 by Connie Gutowsky

Managing Editor: Patrick Grizzell
Graphics Consultant: Liz Ryder Baxmeyer

TULE REVIEW

2023

Editor-in-Chief
Susan Kelly-DeWitt

Cover Artist
Connie Gutowsky

Published by The Sacramento Poetry Center Press
1719 25th Street
Sacramento, California, 95816

sacpoetrycenter.org

In Memoriam Mary McGrath
(July 31, 1942 - April 23, 2023)

This issue of *Tule Review* is dedicated to the memory of our beloved storyteller, Mary Lynne McGrath, who passed away on April 23, 2023. Mary believed in the healing power of storytelling and poetry — she put that belief to work in the world, and we continue to be grateful for her life's work and for her sparkling presence among us.
—Susan Kelly-DeWitt

Photos of Stars and Planets

It's a lost cause now, you know,
finding a dark sky.
Rogue light bleeds everywhere
into the night.

Think of the bloom of stars
in the dark sky,
swirling and shining and
ripening after dusk.
All unseen.

Think of the mating of
Jupiter and Saturn, last seen
by Elizabeth Regina.
Alone in their orbits but
newly engaged, conjoining
on the longest night of the year,
in the majesty of the Winter Solstice.

Think of my mother and father
ecstatic.
Celebrating his return from the War.
Lying on a plaid blanket
in the soft green grass
of her family home.

Basking in starlight, looking up
into the clear dark sky.

Mary McGrath, December 2020

INTRODUCTION

Dear Readers,

    It has been such an honor and pleasure to guest edit the return voyage of Tule Review — to have experienced the depth and breadth of so many wonderful voices, their beauties and complexities. I felt like a traveler sitting on a ship's deck, overlooking a vast sea of imagination — or, like a passenger on a train through a new country —so many interesting details, sightings, personal landscapes enriching my brain.

> *I traveled along*
> *the poems' rich heart and mind*
> *roads — leading us home.*

PS And many thanks to Patrick Grizzell for his input and his tech skills — it couldn't have happened without him!

    — Susan Kelly-DeWitt, Editor

TABLE OF CONTENTS

Introduction   ix

Tom Mitchell   1
   Fields
   Gardening

Andrena Zawinski   2
   Starstruck

Andy Jones   3
   Waves
   Informing the Bones

Ann Privateer   4
   We Are Stardust

Anthony Xavier Jackson   5
   This Old Song

Bob Stanley   9
   Language Barrier

Catherine French   10
   What I Like About Frank
   I Was The Thief

J.C. Olander   12
   The Patio

Chryss Yost   14
   EKG Iconography
   Good and True

Connie Gutowsky   15
   The Talented Fruit

David Weinshilboum 16
    Ginkgo Leaves

Diane Funston 18
    In Freedom

Danyen Powell 20
    Autumnal
    Weather Report

Dianna Henning 21
    The Animals Will Indict Us

Doreen Beyer 22
    Silence of Skylarks

Ed Balldinger 23
    Bound

George Yatchisin 24
    Treasuring Up These Things
    Across The Street

Gillian Wegener 26
    The doctor tells me to pull myself together
    January 1 in the Second Year of the Pandemic

Georgette Unis 28
    A Rune

Gordon Preston 29
    A Walk

John Allen Cann 30
    Postlude
    Scar-Spectacles

Harrie Alley   33
    Poet Moving House
    Beseeching Morpheus

Jack Schouten   34
    Runaway

Jamie Seibel   35
    History Assignment

Jan Haag   36
    The First Law of Thermodynamics
    Holster

Jennifer O'Neill Pickering   38
    Bruised Skies

Jill Stockinger   39
    Cabbage While Butterflies

Julie Bruck   40
    Playground
    Current Climate

Karen DeFoe   42
    Shades of Autumn
    On Carmel Beach

Julie Hannah Brower   44
    Let our rejoicing rise

Laura Garfinkel   45
    A Glimmer

Linda Jackson Collins   46
    Broken Heart
    Burn Scar

Laura King   48
    First Night
    He is A Dune

Linda Toren   50
    Crown Point Rug Auction

Lisa Dominguez Abraham   52
    Americana
    "Art is a tool to create new questions"

Lucille Lang Day   54
    Thinking of Juliane Diller, Who Fell From the Sky
    Past and Future Lives

Lynn Belzer   56
    Capela dos Ossos (Chapel of Bones) 3-14-23

Mary Mackey   58
    Mocking Cassandra

Melinda Rivasplata   59
    Ode to Ceramic Chickens

M.J. Donovan   60
    A Letter to the Empty Jars on the Counter
    Footnotes Under a Photo of a Poet Scowling

Molly Fisk   62
    Decision Tree
    I Was Slicing a Red Pepper

Monika Rose   63
    Reunion

Nanci Woody   64
    A Question for the Gods

Nora Laila Goff   65
    The Poet Shirt

Oswaldo Vargas   66
    The Son of Something

Patricia Wentzel   67
    Serpent's Bite

Paula Sheil   68
    Stone Stone

Randy White   70
    Colonel Liu Draws for Our Daughter
    A Vision

Rachael Ikins   72
    The Cat Wears Secret Messages Rolled in Necklace Scrolls:
        Ars Poetica

Rick Rayburn   73
    Sisyphus Symphony

Sharon Coleman   74
    glow-in-the-dark
    salt

Shawn Pittard   76
    Casting After Shadows
    Reclamation

Sue Daly   77
    All the Love

Susan Flynn   78
    Would You Come If I Called You by Name?
    MARIE

Taylor Graham 81
    Crystal Water

Victoria Dalkey 82
    Sleepwalker
    Kulicke's Orange

Thomas Goff 84
    Sistine Lullaby
    Shakespeare's Own Columbine

Wendy Patrice Williams 85
    Following the Sunlit Trail

Shawn Aveningo-Sanders 86
    Feeding Him Grapes

Alexander Antonio Cortez 88
    Mending Petals

Contributors 90

Thomas Mitchell

Fields

It was hard to leave you at the airport,
and on the way home I noticed
your flowers on the front seat.
It was a long drive, and the fields
and fields of this year's stubble
glistened in the sunlight.

The hay bales were gathered,
trails of crows followed the tractors
pulling dust in the late afternoon.
As I looked into the distance, I thought
this is all we have, short-lived
and then a memory.

Since you left we've had wild huckleberries,
hard rain, and a sudden windstorm. Tonight
it should be clear and I hope to see
a meteor shower, or Andromeda.

Gardening

This morning, doing the hard
root-busting work of turning a yard
from the natural to a gardener's will,
I hear the shrill song of a bird
hidden in the undergrowth,
a *chi chi,* then syncopated
syllables sounding like *find me,*
can you find me here, here
where I am waiting. And finally,
a red and fawn barn finch
appears on the smallest branch
of the Madrone, shaking its head,
then flying off again to who
knows where. Last season's leaves
gather their dark rough edges
around the pond where others
lie submerged in their silence
like shimmering minnows.

Andrena Zawinski

Starstruck

> "My father once said…'you should wait till people are dead to tell stories like that.' Now people are dead and I am telling stories like that."
> — Martín Espada

My father smacked my mother in the breast with a softball
he pitched, a curveball the batter missed in the Pressed Steel
break yard where striking hell-raisers once fought company goons.

Nothing soft about that ball or their meeting as she let out a wail
clutching her chest, tears coursing cheeks as she shrieked "I see stars!"
And as that story goes, it was love at first sight, or so they said.

As he lifted her up from the ground and off her feet as she winced
from pain, it was like some meteor had flown off course to her heart
to make a moment, once you've had it, forgivable and unforgettable.

The rest of their lives would go that way beneath the constellations
of lost jobs and hard luck—Orion tightening the belt at food lines
and welfare visits to check on their two kids in a cold water flat.

A meteor disguised as a baseball brought them together in something
bigger than the two of them could have ever dreamed alone,
        but unlike
Cepheus and Cassiopeia they would not live on together forever.

He got lost gambling, fighting, boozing—roughneck waiting for luck
to turn that never did. After his death she asked, as if I could know:
"What did your father ever see in me?" And I said, as if I knew:
"Stars in your eyes."

Andy Jones

Waves

> *Language is the blood of the soul.*
> — Oliver Wendell Holmes

Drawn by the agonizing air, some first
Devonian fish ached towards tetrapod.
The seaside emerging would dissonate,
choked gasps and sputtering amid the trilobites.
The repeated subsequent instinctive attempts,
the short struggles in that soup of algae,
would be stilled by unyielding fatigue
as the fraught and aspiring hybrids
strung together whispered staccato sequences
of vibrations and reverberations.
Beached and dying amid gravity's pull,
they attempted their first, perhaps our first,
airborne language, frail interruptions
of the itinerant ocean's rumble
before they and their voices were reabsorbed
by the yearning and pounding waves.

Informing the Bones

At some point, we all may all be tempted,
or directed, to unfasten ourselves.
After the recommended surgeries,
the humeri, the patellae,
having gradually decoupled from cartilage,
each with tiny fractures
and x-rayed imperfections,
remained behind in sterile containers.
Drinking from passed flasks
or listening to Donna Summer,
we depended so much upon
those bones we grew,
overseen by grandparents,
until, suddenly, we didn't.
Treated like spurned bees,
nobody told them that their now
marrowless titanium owners had departed.

Ann Privateer

We Are Stardust

Some of us dustier than others
Uniquely made in the shade
Before the sun glimpsed
Our birthday, before remembering,
Before there was a pecking order or
A mind, before Nature, or summer vacations
We became…without a grumble
Or a touch, restlessly pursuing peace
Digging into discovery, naive
To manipulation, like a dragonfly resting
While birds chirp
And stomachs gurgled.

Anthony Xavier Jackson

This Old Song

One day son
We won't have to sing
This same dim song
Malcolm
Huey
Martin
Breonna
George
Trayvon
Emmet
Hampton
Nazarene Son

Someday soon
We can take our
Hands off the bark
Of haunted trees
That scream the names
Of those left swinging
Over fear drenched
Traumatized terrains
In the cruel sideways rain
Of Alabama
Mississippi
Santee California
Kingman Arizona
Tulsa
Dixon
Laredo Texas
The Gold Rush foothills

Any American city
Where you could see
Fascination
Hypnotized little white kids
Stood there
Grinning
As black bodies were twitching
As Black men moonwalked
Above the earth they'd never

Touch again
Eyes fixed to homes
They'd never again see.

You know the song?
How's it begin?
What's the hook?
Where does the chorus blend?
Oh and the change, baby
Where does it ascend?

We've been singing this same song
Too long now son, every day
Every year
Everywhere
We've chanted it in piss stained
Asbestos laden pink project
Stairwells over the clickity
Clack of crack vials
That put clothes on Ronnie Reagan's
Toy soldiers' backs
Hunting communism like
A delusional cat ecstatic
He brought a fried chicken wing back

We sang this song as they drove us
By gunpoint from our berry farms
In the foggy Half Moon Bay
We hummed along as they cuffed
Us on the ground when we
Went to the Santa Cruz Boardwalk
To scream delight and hopefully play
We turned a lapis lazuli blue
Hued by the grey impertinence
Of the electric fences of San Fran
Sunset internment camps
We counted time by the flapping
Wings of ravens over the makeshift
Shacks of Salinas field workers
On the backroads none of the
Beige kids drove
We parlayed the sway of the
Corrugated frames precariously
Balanced on broken pallets

Stolen from the dumpsters
Of McCormick's spice factory
We sang along in the legacy
Museums as our fathers rocked
On shaky legs weighed down
By the flashflood of a million
Runaway slaves gurgling
At the bottom of the ocean
Their noble faces picked clean
By capitalism

One day soon son
The jazz within hip hop
Will melt the faces of
Tiki torch bearing little men
Whose insufficiency
Shaped the welts across
My great grandmother's back
While they stole and stole and stole
For a mink stole on the shoulders
Of indifferent women
Bullied, buried, married into
Complicity in the land of rape
And money, honey it's alright
Just nurse your children with
A black mammy while Massa
Sneaks off in the night
One day soon son we'll retire
That refrain of resentment
Carried over blurred centuries
Disguise the dysfunction
As American Greatness
Classic contentment
Another log on the fire
Another concentration camp
Electric fence

One day soon
Fill your lungs
Son
We'll turn this dread dirt
Field hand skirt

Into the defiant chanting

Of A Love Supreme
While the First Black Woman
President is sworn in

A new song
That strangely
We already know
By
Heart.

Bob Stanley

Language Barrier

From characters on the stone, we know
great-grandfather lies beneath us.

The family's been separated by oceans and politics
for a hundred years, but here we are, sitting on the couch together.
They treat us as if we had never left,
cooking, sharing photos.

As if a long war were over, we are still family.
This is your grandfather's mother,
this is your grandfather's father.
There are a few characters I can recognize.

When we arrived, they set off firecrackers
sending smoke along the concrete alleys.
Now they make us sit, they bring dishes:
peanuts, vegetables, meats, fruit.

Cousins, uncles, aunties, as far removed
as generations across centuries, they keep cooking, clearing,
serving more. The room is hot, the beer warm.
Come see our new staircase, our modern bathroom.

We take the van, they take their small car,
a few mopeds running beside to the new
cemetery on the hill – the one we helped build from far away.
We clamber up through soft soil into the grid of stones.

All this time, the family has been talking.
So much to say, as if there were not enough time.
I have not understood more than a few words,
but I understand almost everything.

Just a few hours, and we move on.

Catherine French

What I Like about Frank
for Frank O'Hara

I suppose I like how it's not as if the world will die
if a line goes wrong the point is to let the day
have its way with you, not fight it or god forbid
not even see it, enjoy it like a party, a constellation
of people appearing like small pinpoints that get
stronger and allow buoyancy, beauty and also mess
an unfinished quality incorporated, embraced even
you can almost feel the molecules getting happy
and lust, how it creeps through the land, the grasses
And because of all this, he levitates sometimes

I Was the Thief

So greedy, taking from everything,
sky, cloud, from the hummingbirds fighting over sugar,
the swaying fragrance of night.
I stole from them all.

Gravity let me stay
on the surface, not fall in
or drift away, rules of physics
I knew nothing about
but stole from nevertheless.
And from the invisible always,
the Great Mother, watching, always giving.

I was the thief, following elemental shine
wherever I went, unlatching the gate
for the horse to escape.
I knew there were rocks
I could break open, find god in.
That lizard tails would come off
in my palm if I dared try
to catch them.

I stole color, sweet and sour,
the sweep of feral beauty - all mine.
Broken things, smoothed by water

and time to an impossibly silken skin.

I declared the whole river mine
just to piss off my brother
who considered it his.

Thistles burrowed in
and I carried them away,
all that wished to be carried,
waiting for me, honoring
the family of thieves.

Holding a light to the lock,
anything to get to the next crime,
subversion or sublime revolution.

Anything to stand again
beneath the waterfall
and feel its constant dissolve
make a long shivering
path through me.

J.C. Olander

The Patio

Yesterday the breezes played chimes
over the flagstone patio—melodies
in long deep resonant tonal rhythms
echoing the cosmic ocean's galaxy
quivering muscles in our bodies.
Yellow leaves from the silver maple
fluttered to the flagstone rock patio
and garden we planted thirty years ago.

Took two years to complete the project:
flagstones laid out in Picasso's cubist style.
Cezanne's bench built in rock retaining wall.
Rockfish descending staircase adds rhythm
and good fire protection until lava rolls over.

It's time for tea on the patio with flowers
surrounding us in pots with your favorite:
pink hibiscus, six-inch diameter petals'
pink deepening to velvet burgundy center
protruding stiff centered stamen sexes it.
We admire the patio garden we created.

"Here, let me help you to the patio table"
I said, as I held you close—we walked out
together on cool stones to sunset memories.
Eurasian Doves peck seeds on the picnic
table as the light fades around us in trees
over the round glass metal table and chairs
for two lovers in the calm evening air
cooling with breezes wafting now and then
trees rustling their dry heat conversations
quickening shadows summer's color pales.

We toast a beer to your birthday, 81 years
then, tour our garden's flowering plants.
Their radiance fleshes thicker, opens brighter
the hibiscus petals' lush, soft, sensuous center
and roses, daisies, daylilies, yarrow, zinnias
columbine, naked ladies, evening primroses.
sphinx moths hovering—hungering for nectar.

We were in love with the world's floral beauty
designs for flowers and trees with vegetables.
We made it complete working beside each other.
"See how the plants flower for us," I said.
"We fed them food they needed," you replied.
We love our garden splashing waves of color.

Now I understand; but, it's time to go back.
The critical hours are approaching quickly.
Helpless to stop time's relentless push I cut
two hibiscuses—one for each of your palms.
Inside the house we built together, we float
each flower in a white and blue bowl of water.
One night with beauty is better than none.
That night you said good-bye to your plants
and your flowers: children for 35 years.

Chryss Yost

EKG Iconography

All doors are entrance and exit at once.

Blood comes in to fist in your ribs,
dark corridors through heart muscle,
valves gasp like a disbelieving mouth.

We look from outside, becoming strange art.

Good and True

That discovery: language that fits between the world and you
the way a camera filter might, so bright, all edges bright, almost
shimmering with its own power. And we hold it for a moment.

How I envy artists, the way they can add more oil, thin it out
when the paint's too thick. Use watercolor. Pastels. The ways
beauty pours from a brush, the forests rise up, the waves, soft
shape of the lovers' jaw, even beheadings become jewel-toned
on the canvas.
              Pity the poet: screen stuck on blank and gray,
nothing radiates out of the keyboard, the letters no better than
a line of ants in their industrious left to right.
                                    Oh, sometimes
these poems think bad, violent things, but there's nothing to do
about it. Holofernes just turns the page, Judith gets even, the
words full of violence, but it doesn't look different enough.
                                                        Next
chapter, the same cockatiels scratch at the page, ready to
rip it to strips, furious, though it looks like a prayer from here.

Connie Gutowsky

The Talented Fruit

I.
The fruit won't ripen, won't spoil, won't draw any gnats.
Life size, luscious, handmade & painted by hand.
The grapes will never rot, nor will the red delicious apples.
soften or shrink, the lemon & lime will stay firm,
the yellow & green pears
always smooth, the guavas exotic. No one will feast on them,
make a sauce or tart out of them, a juice or tonic, or slice them.

II.
The long year is finally over; the anniversary of Al's death is today:
    July 18, 2022.

He was ready to die, put his head on our pillow, closed his eyes,
never opened them again. Now what? Nothing seemed real after that.
I believed I was too young to be a widow at 82, wouldn't wear black.
Death seems like a miracle, like birth. Like meeting Al—his strong
hands, steady gaze, impish at times smile, handsome stride.

Al loved books, loved reading, loved our sons & me; loved teaching,
skiing, hiking, cooking; loved fresh fruit, hated anything *faux*. He
wasn't born to linger, to suffer, to be an old man with Parkinson's.

III.
I can't remember the hard parts, can't stop myself from remembering
the good. They'll never be gone, until I am. I don't feel
sorry for myself.

IV.
I ordered a basket of *faux* fruit. Life-like, in the still-life tradition,
they'll stay ripe & beautiful for years to come.
The cornucopia helps me smile every day.

David Weinshilboum

Ginkgo Leaves

About 40 years ago, my Chinese mother planted a ginkgo tree –
tropical vegetation from her motherland of China—
in the front yard of our Minnesota home.

She dug into the unforgiving earth with both hands
and deposited her diminutive sapling.

It was a pathetic stick embedded in the arctic tundra,
ready to snap against cold, unfamiliar winds.

Oh, how my mother protected that twig
wrapping a cloth wrap around its base,
malleting wood supports against the thin trunk
to keep it warm and vertical.

It was the joke of the neighborhood,
this lifeless piece of wood centered in our lawn.
"How's your mom's stick holding up,"
neighbors would ask, an innocent form
of gallows humor to soften the blow
of the tree's imminent demise.

Yet day after month after year
the tree kept upright, kept going.

It really was a miracle.

In its fledgling years, the leaves — shaped like miniature fans —
would all fall off at once; it took no more than a slam
of the porch door to send its color fluttering groundward.

Every year, my father and I would guess the day the tree
would shed its summer garments and leave a yellow
halo on the green lawn.

Like my mother, that tree has rooted itself deep in the icy grounds
of the Midwest, and today its highest branches are as thick as legs
kicking up toward the cloudless sky.

Its height is beyond any measure my youthful mind

could have ever conjured, and it's outlived many of the
street dwellers who mocked its stature all those years ago.

My mother is old now; her legs—as frail as the infant ginkgo's trunk—
will never step foot outside Minnesota again.

When I walk these California streets I'm surrounded
by displaced ginkgos; their yellowing leaves look at me
earnestly, like my mother's eyes regarding me
from under her bifocals, a quiet salute before they break from
their branches and descend softly to ground.

Diane Funston

In Freedom

There is freedom in flight
to places I've not seen.

A pet raven rests
in the Tower of London.

Voodoo spirits haunt
old graves in New Orleans.

An oryx on the African Savannah
impales a lion on saber sharp horns.

There is freedom in flight
to places I've seen.

Oscar Wilde's ghost laments his love
in Père Lachaise Cemetery.

Dresden's domed church stands again
from bricks and sweat long after the bombs.

Niagara's force pours full range of emotion
despite the garish river of tourists.

There is freedom in flight
inward, back home to the soul.

Where we return to our beginnings
welcomed by our own outstretched arms.

We begin again right where we are,
a chance to get it right this time.

Not a moment to undo years of neglect,
more a lifetime to polish the stone lovingly.

There is freedom in flight
outward, in meeting others of our tribe.

Connection, recognition of linking minds

whether in person or computer screen.

Electric currents of desire perhaps,
a button undone, flirtatious invitation.

Words stringing us together for a time
then landing on paper for posterity.

Freedom is in the discovery,
Foreign
Familiar
Me
You
Us

In flight together.

Danyen Powell

Autumnal

demolished storefronts

the forgotten

line the sidewalks

murmur

in the brittle leaves

Weather Report

massive
        low front

wet leaf
            stuck
to the bottom of your soul

bring an umbrella

expect
     a relentless downpour
of shrapnel

Dianna Henning

The Animals Will Indict Us

With burnt paws, some with flames riding bareback,
bears raced down mountainsides,
pines crackling, trunks snapping,

the unholy terror of destruction, flames
engulfing trees, vegetation, animals,
ground and rocks blackened
into vestments priest's wear—

the stench of ash as though all of earth
was burial ground   and perhaps so,
death upon the dead, mounds of them,
the aching back of earth weighted with so many bones,
what to do with so many,

and who'll cry for the land, the animals, the people,
who'll extinguish the harm wrought,
or right balance with a good shepherd's eye?

Doreen Beyer

Silence of Skylarks

The distant grumble of explosions, earth gouged by demonic
tungsten-tipped claws, jet fuel-fed flames dwindle

the natural and human landscape to black, smoking ruins—
an act of slow devouring.

Winter approaches this terrain of hardships in shivering lights
of candles, hard beam of flashlights, in firewood collected…

ground-nesting Gray Partridge—coveys condemned
to a subtraction of loneliness, or else

to roast on makeshift stoves—wily Black Kite, once
a sacred bird, drops a firebrand to areas unburnt—

flushes out what prey remain—the joyous offering
of a skylark's long song, sung only in flight,

gone in a gridlock of drones, missiles and artillery.
In the approaching dawn, threads of ragged smoke

ascend like ghosts (*like broken-winged birds*) haunting
a world, without their song.

Ed Balldinger

Bound

I'm a blank sheet of paper
in a binder amid ten thousand words.
I'm the final sentence minus punctuation and
I'm ready to be etched in a story that never begins.

I'm a lock of hair on the floor beneath
an electric chair that was once used
for an illicit complicity back in the 1930's.
I walk through tight-knit shadows unrestrained –
there is no light by which I am lit.

I see the Sierra wave up high -
the sky of the valley
where mad men rave;
I see clown carcasses
draped in worn-out skin.
I walk side by side
with who we are again.

He's over the limit
I'm under the line.
She's into the river
and I'm all outta wine!

I'm a third of a sheet that is blown in the wind,
torn from a binder I thought was my friend,
but now I tumble and flutter
wherever the breeze will take me…

There's a danger in embracing irreversible time.
There's safety in possessing no clock.

I'm a blank sheet of paper
absent of horrific news that
defines our own disconnection.

So, slip those velvety ropes around my wrists,
tie my feet to a twisted May pole and sling
undocumented words against my broken shield
where I sit bound to my own absence of truth.

George Yatchisin

Treasuring Up These Things

The satisfying sproing the tight coil of the ox's horn made—
a sound just past silent—if you flicked it just right.
How the crook Joseph held in his little statue hand
was metal, practically a straightened paper clip,
and you could pull it completely from his proud fatherly grip,
then worry about how the trouble would come if he lost it.

That corrugated cardboard, waffly box it was stored
and no doubt bought in, with "Made in Italy" inked on top,
as mythical as Bethlehem to a five-year-old suburban boy.
The wooden slat crèche inside also a box with a flap that folded out
to set theatrical parameters for one to set up the Nativity play.

Did the straw inside hold the scent of the attic's dust or
of the stalks of cereal plants dead and of another country?
More fascinating to the boy was the straw's duo of uses—
first packing, where the holy statues slept till each holiday season,
then to be their manger bedding—first safety, then mere setting.

How old was he when he learned it was more interesting to place
the Holy Family a bit off to the side, angled to accept both shepherds
and kings bearing gifts that made no sense in an infant's world.
How much better, if hard to admit, to let the world be less centered,
let the donkey bathe directly under the star's sparkle that wasn't more,
alas, than one bulb from the tree hung above the manger
to push the story along, only in the best years truly lambent.

Across the Street

Your poor neighbor whose wife's cancer came back,
the guy who might vote Trump and surfs and restored
his woody to California brilliance and is in AA
and still probably drinks—as you would drink,
as you drink—he sees your anniversary post
for your wife where you found a poem so fine
from someone else you quote it whole and
you realize that neighbor might even think
it's yours, and he says, "I should have done
that more for Suzanne." But of course she's dead,
but of course he needs more than you or
anyone can give him, which is her, again.
And even if you could, he wouldn't quote
her poems. We mean so well without learning.

Gillian Wegener

The doctor tells me to pull myself together

He's listening to me talk of headaches that I wake up with and go to sleep with, headaches that keep me home from school. Tall, white coat, wearing sneakers, not unkind. He tells me this is capital S stress and I just need to deal with it. I just need to pull myself together, but no instructions are provided. He's not being harsh, just matter of fact. At home, I am nursing two hummingbird nestlings with an eyedropper and sugar water, their nest a soft hollow, their mouths wide open. They are solace, not stress. I gave them names and I love them, but sugar water is not what they need, and I am not their mother who is out there somewhere, maybe mourning her feathered losses. The doctor doesn't ask about this and I don't tell him. Also, no one asks about or tells the causes of stress. They remain undefined, unarticulated, unattached to any real thing. Which makes it easy to say, silly girl, just pull yourself together. Bootstraps, and no other instructions. Just change it. Just deal with it. The hummingbirds died, first one, beak closed, then the other, sugared and slumped. Just deal (on your own) with it. We bury them under the orange tree. I go to school even though my head hurts. I pull myself together. At least for the short term. These little deaths are inevitable. I pocket the stress. I deal with it. At least as far as (shhh) anyone knows.

January 1 in the Second Year of the Pandemic

On this morning's walk,
I wish everyone Happy New Year
but I'm thinking, *what a hypocrite.*
I'm thinking the word *happy* is a deflating balloon.

We pass someone else with a puppy.
She says, *Today's just like yesterday,*
and I get it, but her puppy is wearing
a shock collar. He sits when she says sit.

Our puppy runs in circles and barks
at anyone on a scooter. Yesterday,
today, and tomorrow -- the same fears.

Our hair gathers the fog.
Someone has spray-painted
R U Happy Now? on the path.

We pass the same people mostly:
the man with his taped-together hand weights,
the woman who is scared of dogs.
We've given them backstories.

We pass the same trees.
They don't need backstories. They have
their oak galls and persimmons.
The lucky ones have oranges.

Our dog hates crossing the street
and waits until one of us ventures out first.

I say *Happy New Year*
and kind of hate myself.

On the path, someone has spray painted
Sorry, Cookie.

Georgette Unis

A Rune

In a dream of houses, a mossy green roof
buckles over a bent rain gutter. No water flows

in this flat image with no vanishing point, a term
for drawing, a term for the end of everything so far

in the future we forget its implications, but for those
of us who time has worn weary, it becomes

a message to rue. The house stands without foliage
or company, equivocal as an ancient oracle.

If every dream mirrors aspects of ourselves, then
I need once again to plant orange and yellow poppies

amidst succulents with brilliant pink blossoms,
rows of hibiscus and maple trees, leaves vermillion

in autumn, branches silvered grey as I approach winter.
I would open the shades, light the desk inside,

chronicle days I ran barefoot through grass,
hiked over Crystal Crag in the Sierra mountains,

and paint images of forests, mountains, rivers and deserts
welcoming my presence.

Gordon Preston

A Walk

The first quarter mile
under a sorrowful
early January sky
steps labored and
labored breathing
best to take the dive
into meanderings

two doves
avoiding a scrub jay
a car crunching over
red hackberries
littering the street
and me walking away
from a COVID pneumonia
that just won't count
as a dance
in anyone's eyes

except a bird on the wire
an egg in a basket
a dinnerplate
Woodland Spode
capturing winter awe
on wings far overhead that we
can almost imagine to see.

John Allen Cann

Postlude

I won't be the last one
puzzling into the strange particulars
of his busy life, buttoned up
& dwelling on Penitence Lane.

If I take the time to put pen to paper,
I must forget he's already said
what I'll have to say. His rhapsodies
of dread & enervation
circumscribe our curious souls.

I know if I met him with his bowler on,
appointed like a banker
rising through the ranks,
I would shake his hand in a formal way
as if an agent of Thanatos & Hay.

I would know not to ask
what he did for 'fun'
or if there was any of his youth
he cared to share.

His smile, indecipherable,
would put me at ease
with just a hint
he knew what I would never understand.

And now we would get down
to the cheese of things,
how time ages some things well
while others take on a rancid smell.

All the while I'd be beguiled
by his probity & the scope
of his restraint, until
we took our leave in the rain,
opening our umbrellas
at the same time,
heading in opposite directions
down Penitence Lane.

Scar-Spectacles

Sooner or later, like it or not,
he finds himself
wearing his scar-spectacles,
through which the childhood
he cannot outrun
twists everything into dark shapes
of painful memories.

What once happened to him
shapes how he sees things now,
he's always coming up short
when the scar-specs
are on his nose.

Everyone owns a pair of scar-spectacles,
though some may seldom need to put them on,
some can't bear the world without them,
& some would like an extra pair,
others wish to forget where they last left them.

His better-half says she misplaced her scar-specs,
though they've been on her nose all along.
Often while wearing them, she hears certain voices:
verbal taunts still sting
when the scar-spectacles are in use.

Now & again the scar-specs
appear on my face,
unbidden,
often during an inward look;
I peer through lenses
of hurt, failure & misjudgment,
& the pain tangles me
in the hard web
of wounds.

How do you get past childhood wounds
when you've worn the scar-specs
for so long, it's disorienting
to take them off?

A rare person you would be

who doesn't have them on
recalling what cost you
your innocence.

With scar-spectacles,
sometimes what hasn't happened yet
already is taking the shape
of something far in the past
that meets you wherever you're going.

Harrie Alley

Poet Moving House

I cannot write any poems!
My hands have fallen off and scuttled away.
They must have gone into the largest cardboard packing box
Among the fragile goblets, each turned into a padded lump
Encased in layer upon layer of bubble wrap.
My hands must be in there somewhere
Down near the bottom of the box
Under balls of crushed newspaper
Or those odious, indestructible plastic packing peanuts.
I cannot hold a pen
But at least there in that box my hands will be protected.
I hope they will not give up on me and disappear somewhere.
When there is an opportunity I trust they will return…
Perhaps when someone unwraps a goblet,
Fills it with cool well water, and
Offers it to quench my thirst.
Then perhaps they will wriggle up out of the packing chaos
With poems in their grasp to help me accept the water,
Help me toast the great oak trees,
The neon ruby and sage green hummingbirds darting among them,
Assist me offering libation
To grey squirrels and red headed woodpeckers.
Oh, *then* I will be done with moving house!

Beseeching Morpheus

I thump my pillow, despairing of sleep; I wilt
Exhausted, wishing the clock face would crack and break
In half. I've tried all known tricks for the sake
Of courting sleep, my earnest efforts bilked
Of success. The dratted sheep *drank* my warm milk!
Still I chase them along corridors of wake
Struggling to count, though tired eyes and body ache.
I yearn for the dreaming world that slips like silk

Where a rippling stream remembers my sandbox pail
Where little neon fish marvel at my toes
Where under a hot, blue sky tree shadows flow
And wish finds a ruined marble temple, veiled
In mystery-- an allegoric tale
Wherein days remember what dreams already know.

Jack Schouten

Runaway

He has no time to go. Circumspect and circumstance
Dictate to him a quality of loss he feels

More than understands. The cans of chili,
Tuna, and soup make up for him a diet of piety,

Punishment enough for the house's one can opener
He pilfered in thinking ahead for his new-found homelessness.

His thinking repeats back to him while urban hiking
Among those he imagines began this way, his way,

Refusing a parent life that no longer makes sense,
He'll make do, find out on his own those boundaries

Mom & dad readymade for him, a kind of stitching,
Twin philosophies of the have and hold variety,

Meant for his safety and well-being he will now
Practice and measure on his own until laughed at

By some wheelchair Pete, or scoffed to think
This life is that easy by a toothless Martha.

They follow him around, even now as he tries to
Sleep back home after this would-be residency

With the indigent who have no choice, who
Remind him to behave and brush his teeth,

To understand he has a choice in all this even when
Really he has no option at all, save to just do until what he does

Becomes automatic, accepted, where he can make
A life of his own w/out fear, w/out frustration.

Tule 34 Review

Jamie Seibel

History Assignment

I did not want to write
about the 1911 fire,
or the 146 workers
who lost their lives,
or the 10 stories
it took to end them.
I wish I could write
about happier things
than young Jewish girls
stitching, sewing with
prickled-numb fingertips
on the rows of machines
and wooden cutting tables.
The hours spent making
sleeves and buttonholes
even on hot, sweaty
summer days.
I did not want to think
about that day in March,
when the flames spread
in a manner of seconds,
or the screaming, pushing,
shoving, as they stampeded
like herds of cattle to elevators,
windows, balconies, searching
for any means of escape,
finding themselves
standing on a ledge
with their cinder-soot faces
overlooking a salmon sky
and having no choice
but to fall.

Jan Haag

The First Law of Thermodynamics

No energy gets created in the universe,
and none is destroyed.

So although his physical body lies stilled,
breathless, or she who still lives sits vacant,
absent without leave, a shell of her former self,

the photons that careened from their smiles,
the electricity of their touch,
their energy goes on forever—

not just in you, who carries their DNA,
the color of their eyes, their very cells
in your own—

but they exist forever in the universe
along with trillions of other particles
that yours will one day join.

It's the law of conservation of energy:
Nothing comes to be or perishes.
The energy we imagine as ours
does not belong to us; we belong to it,
transformed from one form into another.

There is no *there*, no *here*.

In the end we are all simply rearranged,
our atoms repurposed, ping-ponging
through space with all those who
ever lived—humans, leaves, amoeba—

some who breathed and walked upright,
who occupied the forms in which we loved them
for not nearly long enough.

Holster

When you came toward me for a hug,
your mother's casket a few feet away crowned with
her favorite roses, shadowed in summer morning shade,
I circled you with arms that had once embraced
a different kind of heat.

It was brief, your new wife observing nearby, and polite,
but I felt the forgotten shape of your undergarment beneath
the loose black shirt draped over the hanger of your shoulders,
and my heart recoiled like the trigger under your armpit,
remembering *oh, yes, this is why*—one reason anyway.

Knowing how it frightened me, long ago when you came to visit,
you stashed the thing in your truck before you entered
my house, my bed, me.

But what scared me more was how much I wanted you then,
even with so much firepower and coiled anger at hand,
you so convinced that you had to have it strapped to you
at all times, except with me.

At the time I did not see it for the sacrifice it was,
the act of a heart trying to be generous, how you would
lay down your weapon to hold me, imagine for a night
that you did not have the means to kill, only to love,
and I pretended right along with you.

Jennifer O'Neill Pickering

Bruised Skies

She thinks of their colliding,
a forgetting into soft tangles,
blood sealed beneath cellophane of skin,
hearts that thrum as one.

Charmed bracelets ring her wrists.
Music follows the hedge of orange azaleas.
Tears cloud eyes perfect as pearls.
It is a time of bruised skies, of waiting.

Unexpected rain falls,
heavy, unforgiving.
Bones stir, surface, where they do not belong.
Dog's ears twitch long before arrivals.

Burgundy unleashes fruity breaths.
Candles taste with flamed tongues.
The sweet bread refuses to rise,
sinks back into itself.
Fists unfold, repair the undoing.

Jill Stockinger

Cabbage White Butterflies

I found a quiet, secluded, rarely used
path to the river. It was overgrown
by bushes and blackberry brambles, thick
with weeds, green and brown everywhere.
I moved slowly down the narrow path
carpeted with coarse grass. There were
tiny yellow flowers of oxalis, bindweed
twining up small saplings, nutsedge, fleshy
purslane, mustard, nettles and showy ferns.
The air was filled with the fragrance of small
spring flowers and other growing things.
Suddenly I was enclosed in hoops of small
white butterflies. I walked through them.
They fluttered, circling around and over
me, churning, a living welcoming nave
all the way to the rocks lining the river.
They left as abruptly as they had come.
It left me breathless and wondering.

Julie Bruck

Playground

Last time I walked by it was deserted.
Same tubular structures the two girls
learned to climb on, swing, and slide.
First, as egg-shaped toddlers we mothers
had to spot, hands tensed in case they faltered.

When they grew longer and leaner we could
sit and talk nearby, while they sped, hand
over hand, a confidence we cheered.
But yours was the one who *flew*—who pumped
every swing to the limit, until the whole frame

trembled as you tried to talk her down.
She was fearless, your girl, born that way,
so different from her careful friend, my own
soft child. By thirteen, Circus School, where
we watched her in fuschia tights, sequins,

her face a made-up mask, one leg fastened
by a strap spinning her sixty feet overhead,
those joints so hyper-mobile doctors tested
for a syndrome she turned out not to have.
We feared for her, and soon, when nothing seemed

to give her any pleasure, we began to fear her.
You let her go at sixteen, to live with that other family
across the Bay: at first, she sounded settled.
You wanted her happy. You needed her gone,
this child who came home only to kick out

the living room windows, so laced with piercings
and heavy chains she clanked into every room
like a threat. You bought her a pit-bull for protection.
She burned through Santa Cruz, Humboldt County,
Ohio, Colorado. Each place, another house-fire,

arrest, pregnancy, a trailer shared with the boyfriend,
swept away by flood. Her Instagram was a wishlist
of assault weapons, spiked clubs, fixed-blade knives.
You always wired money when she asked.

We fear for our children. Sometimes, we fear them.

You thought you'd been funding the boyfriend's
welding classes, another fresh start in a new place.
I knew this would happen—was all my daughter could
repeat, an endless loop, the day I called to tell her.
I knew it. I knew! And I told you—

Current Climate

The scanner breaks. We order another.
Sonoma's on fire, second time this month.
On Sunday, we pamphlet houses in Daly City.
It gets so hot we have to quit, tote bags still
bulging with flyers. Plus, our friend—tall,
black and male—feels profiled, uneasy
in that part of town. The modem quits.
We cancel today's meetings, tonight's classes.
A replacement ships, but there's no firm
delivery date. Our upstairs neighbors
lend us two air filters while they're away,
let us park in their garage. They're back,
so our car's outside again, coated in ash.
We return their machines. Try to buy our own,
but they're back-ordered, due to unprecedented
demand. You know, wildfires, Covid 19,
locusts. The present's such a relentless tense.
Just in case there's a future, rain can fill
the aquifers, overwhelm the city's drains
until every street is choked by vans from *Ace,
Chosen, Friendly, 24/7* or *Roto Rooter*, each spilling
out its plumber to greet their former competitors
as brethren once more—members of a single
union, high-fiving each other like crazy.

Karen DeFoe

Shades of Autumn

> *Season of mists and mellow fruitfulness!*
> — John Keats

thief of summer
bitter sweetness nesting in the trees
silent shadow mother
too early sending a reluctant summer sun to bed
shrinking daylight hours   bit by bit   day by day
harbinger of hibernation
do not sing me your lullaby
I cannot dream you away
like ladybugs hiding in windowsills or
hedgehogs burrowed underground
I cannot take night flight with the twittering swallows
I am not ready for sleep in the underworld
glorious encore before the dying light
sing me your nostalgic love song
sing of goddesses
weaving their plaits of amber hair
dancing beneath the tangerine glow of your harvest moon
herald of harvest
offer up your conciliatory gifts
your *mellow fruitfulness*   rich and ripe
orange-fleshed pumpkins   blushing apples
crisp woodsy pears   sweet purple plums
bring me nosegays of daisies and violas   bunches of sunflowers
bouquets of   lilies   dahlias   chrysanthemums
let color riot   adorn the birches with golden coins
ignite the maples   let their leaves flame   orange   crimson
burgundy
set bush and briar ablaze   brilliant golds   rusts   magentas
and
before the colors fade to brown
and
before your breath blows bare the boughs and scatters leaves
call forth the robin's whistled carol   the woodpecker's tatting knock
and
let their music comfort me as I grieve
the cold   slow   dying of the year

On Carmel Beach

in mid-July   the hungry seagulls
fly above the curl and roll of waves   soaring
scanning   gliding   diving
into the salty spray to catch
and feast on unsuspecting prey that
in the open water cannot hide
and I
soothed from sun and salty breeze
as lazy afternoon begins to wane
listen to the raucous cries disperse
above the swelling waves
and raise
my glass of chardonnay to toast
the ocean's rhythmic sighs
as evening sun bows
to pastel sky.

Julie Hannah Brower

Let our rejoicing rise

Cracked gate lolls on one hinge
sun worn, moisture long dissipated
thin grey splinters that will break off under winter's drifts
Over time its arc narrows
Where once a fat black cow could pass
now only a doe grazing on the last of summer's green might fit
Fawns trailing behind slip through
A rock, no bigger than an egg laid by the smallest hen
nestles against a gate post
rolled, jolted to a stop
unmoved since its arrival
Curly pillbugs, tiny spiders shelter near the rock in spring and summer
bustle away when days begin to cool
Passers-by–the few there are–do not see the rock
though once, a girl–curious enough about the gate
to brush her fingertips along its rusty hinges
peel the faded maroon paint, drop flakes on to a nearby ant hill
and watch them scurry–
was so close that the big toe on her right foot nearly scuffed the rock

One day when the girl is much older, filled with city life, books
a husband, she'll pass by the gate
now only remnants of two posts, barely upright
She'll glance down, curl her fingers around a rock
slip it into her left front pocket
In the gate's opening she'll stretch her
arms wide, sing   Faintly, at first
unused to making sound, then louder, rumbly, a
gay creek over stones and fallen branches   Finally, she'll
remember the song her father sang at night, supper
over, dishes washed, homework done   He
didn't sing to her, exactly, though they were always
in the same room when he began   She
sat quietly then, closed her eyes, felt the loose
strings of day pull close, tie neatly together
two thin loops each like the crescent moon

Laura Garfinkel

A Glimmer

> *Teach us to Number Our Days that we may get*
> *a heart of wisdom*
> — Psalm 90

Too soon, the day gets later and the light dims.
Like trying to capture the moon in a bucket of water,
your thoughts on paper — some rhythm, meter,
a few reflections and memories. A glimmer
of your time here, fleeting, yet repeating cycles.
Now, you are the older neighbors on the block;
young families move into vacated homes.
A friend's grandchild asks, *What is death?*
Can you show me on your phone?
My friend shows her a picture of a bee on its back,
legs straight up, wings spread. I've learned
a bee can shoot venom after death
if you step on it. I want to go as quietly
as that bee, wings spread until the end,
a little sting left behind.

Linda Jackson Collins

Broken Heart

Imagine the worst. The unwanted buildup
of proteins in your brain, tau tangles and plaque

like the kind a hygienist scrapes from your teeth.
Imagine that crusty stuff fracturing

neural pathways, making strangers of friends,
blackening memory's movie screen.

Your life's landscape broken
into jigsaw puzzle pieces.

Now imagine that *doesn't* happen:
that your mind understands every

word of your doctor's diagnosis.
That it conjures up vivid pictures

of shriveled prunes,
and the last measure of air sputtering

from a deflated balloon.
Your doctor offers little comfort

and you imagine her thinking
a 90 year-old heart is lucky to beat at all.

But you don't feel so lucky,
remembering your sister's

blue fingertips grasping at handrails,
her gurgling voice.

You imagine a protective layer
of plaque might not be so bad.

Maybe you wouldn't notice
a nasal cannula, a tightened chest.

Maybe you wouldn't be so scared.

Burn Scar

Stillness in the forest.
                        Autumn breeze.

       Before, we couldn't see
            through the thicket,
     couldn't feel solid ground
              beneath the pine needle mat.

Leafless branches pierce the sky,
                    an accusation.

There is so much we didn't hear.
Who atones for warnings waved away
                        like smoke?

A woman snaps through brittle brush.
                  Ash billows underfoot.
She lops wounded boughs and drags
them into roadside piles.

     It won't be enough.

Moss covers a charred stump.
                  Sprigs emerge from scorched bark.
We fool ourselves again and again.

Something new will grow here
                  but it will be much changed
long after blackened trunks fall.

Laura King

First Night

The holidays almost expired,
lights in our neighborhood
masquerading as stars.

I'll miss them when they're gone.

We awoke this first morning,
knowing it would be your last.
You'll have other mornings,
but no more new years.

We are done pretending.

Tomorrow there will be boxes,
ladders, deceased decorations
dismantled, extension cords unplugged.

I will have the lonely stars
aloof in the heavens, as I
walk long dark winter alone.

He Is A Dune

morphine drip
        strips his upper consciousness
grains
        sliding down the slipface
the way sand creeps
        up the stoss and glides
down the lee
        until the wind reverses

                      drifting out
drifting in

then his mother
        old friends and revenants

he returns
        with glittered visions

It is not like in the beginning
        where the soul pushes into light

he experiments with going

    the way sand is turned to mark time

        falling through
and back again

    it is hard to know where death begins
like a sea
    sandhill
        or shore

Linda Toren

Crown Point Rug Auction

Weavers make their way
from homes that might have
running water, electricity
but probably no phone.

Each carries a basket
laden with rugs—
Tree of Life, Two Grey Hills,
Sand paintings.

Long skirts sway
like ghosts across
high desert paths,
ancient sheep trails.

A young girl carries
her first rug.
Old women herd her
into the vast room.

Rugs with number tags
cover cafeteria tables—
scent of sour milk
lingers in the background.

Buyers from around the world
lift, touch, look at the quality
of designs, write down numbers,
sit with a number plate in lap.

I am looking for red,
the kind of red
that leans toward purple.
It is rare since the little beetles
can only be collected
once during the year,
preparation arduous,
recipe handed down
weaver to weaver.

These old women know
the old ways—
herd the sheep,
gather the wool,
card it, spin it,
dye with colors
of earth and sky.

Red is a blessing
not just because it's rare—
blood of the Dine people.

Red is connected to
all life, pulse with it—

the young girl
reluctant to sell
her first rug,

newly weds
who will buy one
to last a lifetime,

Germans who look like
FBI agents will sell the rugs
at inflated prices.

Ghostly figures rise
from the earth

yei be chei
magenta in their spirit regalia.

Lisa Dominguez Abraham

Americana

Sacramento, you were a claustrophobia
of tree-lined streets. Even when I climbed
my roof, your screen of leaves blocked my view,
so I learned to look street-level.

>   I rode shotgun in a pickup between rows
>   of orange trees, flinching as blasts
>   and high-fives from the pickup bed
>   punctuated crows dropping into the dust.

I tried the local diner where conversation
stopped when my sons and I stepped in,
too brown and not from here. Bacon hissed
on the griddle. The air blinked. We stepped back.

>   I tried to see our neighborhood as a children's book
>   sketched with camellias and endless lawns,
>   where couples leashed to dogs and strollers
>   waved to others on bicycles. I learned

the cadence of Little League—Slide! Slide!
and my boys grew into muscled little guys
who wore dirt-smeared jerseys and spat
sunflower shells like pros.

>   Later, alone, I found behind chain link fence
>   an alley cottage where writers drank red wine,
>   smoked good pot, and invited me
>   to talk out ideas, to trust my own eyes.

Sacramento, you shortened my view
so I looked up and saw the torn black paper
of crows chasing a hawk, their tableau backlit
by sunset, maples rustling autumn.

>   Because of you I know better, now,
>   the rest of my country, and I'll leave
>   with your good-bye branded like a kiss
>   a lover once seared into my palm.

"Art is a tool to create new questions"
— Ai Weiwei

A woman's toddler plays beneath her chair
as she paints a porcelain sunflower seed

with precise gray swipes. Her job pays
by the kilo so that untold kilos of seeds

can be spread in a museum,
an expanse that patrons can cross

only in imagination. Looking closer they see
each seed is nearly uniform,

the gray of a janitor's coveralls
or aprons worn by two women

lugging a vacuum and spray bottles
into a two-story house. The gray is water

speckling a rest home attendant
as he gentles an elder into a shower,

droplets arcing behind a gardener
mowing the golf course at 7 a.m.

At the launch party, guests celebrate the artist
with a signature cocktail: salt-rimmed glasses,

pepper-infused gin. Framed plaques thank
the porcelain miners and painters

who, supporting their families
with piecework, made his vision possible.

They're toasted en masse, from afar,
as a custodian discreetly mops a spilled drink,

her children's initials tattooed on her wrist.

Lucille Lang Day

Thinking of Juliane Diller, Who Fell from the Sky

If a seventeen-year-old girl can fall 10,000 feet
when a plane breaks in two

and embrace the silence that surrounds her
when the other passengers cease to scream

If she can spin downward, noticing how trees
look like broccoli and the world is all green

and land in the Amazon rainforest of Peru
still strapped into her row of seats

If she can wake the next day with a concussion,
broken collarbone, and gashed shoulder and knee

and hear a band-tailed manakin whistle
while black-capped squirrel monkeys shriek

If she can walk, wade, and swim, following
rivers and streams, barefoot, in a tattered minidress

and hike past three passengers, still buckled in,
planted headfirst in the forest floor

If she can keep going, past eight-foot caimans,
scorpions, spiders, and poisonous snakes

and survive on water and a small bag of candy
while her wounds fester with maggots

If she can reach civilization in eleven days
and make saving the rainforest her life's work,

then whenever we're alone and something
has gone terribly and irrevocably wrong

and the rescue planes have stopped circling,
surely we can muster the guts to push on

Past and Future Lives

> *Simple statistics reveal that your body contains about one atom of carbon from every milligram of dead organic material more than a thousand years old...*
> — Paul R. Fleischman, *Wonder*

You are partly Jesus Christ and Buddha,
men who humbly tended the sick and taught
forgiveness, also Cleopatra, Atilla the Hun
and Nero, a Roman emperor remembered
for wasting money, burning Rome in order
to rebuild it, plotting his mother's murder,
and killing his first and second wives.

You contain the dinosaurs that ruled Earth
for more than one hundred million years,
the yews and cypresses they consumed,
and the birds they gave rise to, which rose
in turn as Audubon's oriole with a black
hood and yellow back, the gray vireo,
and chipping sparrow with its rusty cap.

About three percent of your genes are unique
to mammals. The rest you share with figs
and fish, crocodiles, crocuses, and even
the one hundred trillion tons of bacteria
teeming in soil and water, thriving on skin,
and turning sugar into lactic acid in the guts
and urinary tracts of other living things.

What essential messages will your life carry
into the future of insects and silken flowers
you will never see? You'll give them carbon,
hydrogen, and oxygen, a reactive nonmetal.
You are everything that ever lived on Earth
or ever will, alive thanks to forces and quarks
and the photons that light up green leaves.

Lynn Belzer

Capela dos Ossos (Chapel of Bones) 3-14-23

> Above the chapel door, a sign reads
> "we bones, are here, waiting for yours."
> --Atlas Obscura

During your last autumn we toured
Portugal at a slower pace, providing
time to enjoy the country and each other.

Long, lingering lunches,
views of broad vistas beyond
I sat next to you, rather than across,

taking time to bask in your glow,
as though we had forever,
you never acknowledging your dimming.

We explored historic hill towns, each with
sharp streets, each clutching their history
and their surviving inhabitants.

You marveled at an elderly woman, darkly
dressed, climbing laboriously up a steep hill
toward a black Mercedes waiting at the top.

This was a different kind of trip. Nothing fancy.
Good food, quiet hotels and streets, outdoor
art, tender walks.

You were our driver, I our guide.
Pre-recorded GPS, thick English accent,
making us hoot at British road jargon.

We lodged outside the walls of Evora,
known for its Chapel of Bones.
You were mesmerized by their mass.

I hesitated before entering,
resisting your enthusiasm
and the chill of death within.

Our last stop was Sintra. Pine-
covered hills, a Moorish castle
on top, I wanted to linger there.

Shortly after Portugal you began to fade
more quickly, taking our future with you,
leaving me to tend to my heart's crevasse.

Mary Mackey

Mocking Cassandra

they mocked her when she said
cities would go under
rocks melt   oceans boil
birds fall from the sky
beaches be ankle-deep in green foam

they laughed at her for laying in stores
filling cans with water
called her crazy   cracked
drove her from town to town like Mirabai
in rags with a begging bowl

when she kept crying   look! it's getting closer!
wet bulb 35C!   brownouts!   blackouts!
famine!   war!   pestilence!
people cooked in their beds!
they shook their heads   rolled their eyes
put Airpods in their ears   watched the playoffs
bought virtual genitals and hooked up in the Metaverse
ate potato chips and smoked weed
shot up high schools
and took photos of their cats playing the piano

poor, crazy Cassandra, they said
hypervigilant, hysterical, neurotic
get her a therapist   shove pills down her throat
Ativan, Celexa, Lexapro, Zoloft
the whole fucking cocktail
just shut her up   she's spoiling the party

but she could see darkness
running around the rim of the horizon
see the light blurring
see the end of dishes washed by machines
contrails   ice cubes
the easy way you could call people
on the other side of the planet
hear their voices   see their faces
tell them you loved them

Melinda Rivasplata

Ode to Ceramic Chickens

There are two.
Hatched from a plaster cast in mother's
converted-henhouse studio near the barn
set back from the red dirt road. Necks arched,
heads bent toward one another. Gleaming
white feathers, red combs and wattles,
reflective metallic-glazed dark tail feathers.
The rooster with a tall red comb,
the hen with a red flower on her breast.

They roosted across the west
in china cupboards, on bookshelves,
sideboards, mantels, dressers.
They stoically occupied
farmhouses and modest homes.
They survived each relocation
and the close calls of dust cloths
activated by Saturday morning chores.

They gazed on whiteout snowfall and
day-darkening dust storms, children
playing dominoes and teens moaning
over algebra homework. They roosted
next to the clay-laced ballerina figurine
that did not survive to see California.

They are with me still.
Now that I grow old, I realize they are still older.
Always there to silently cluck and crow,
to let me know this is home.
If I had to leave today with just one
token of those times
I would take those chickens.
Faithful still.

M.J. Donovan

A Letter to the Empty Jars on the Counter

Wide-mouth masons; hexagonal green glass; repurposed turmeric
jar; 1970 spice rack set with glass corks—now three short;
grandma's glass cookie jar; 2-quart sun-tea jar; spaghetti sauce
and marmalade jars rescued from recycling, labels scrubbed off,
dishwasher sanitized; aquamarine salve jars; cranberry juice jar;
antique milk of magnesia bottle:

How do you hold emptiness with such luminescence?
Light passes through you like a cold stream,
all sediment settled.

I envy your shadow. Give me a translucent body
—every angle untethering a new refraction.

What do you do when they fill you with cumin
and stuff a cork in your mouth?

Can you teach me to remember the light, even then?

Footnotes Under a Photo of a Poet Scowling

Warning: This poet is not dangerous
though the furrowed brow
convinces otherwise.

Caution: Any attempt to photograph
will result in a furrowed brow.

Definition: Furrowed brow =
confusion, boredom, surprise,
loss of sure footing,
hunger, sleepiness, irritation,
and sometimes—anger.

Clarification: Anger is not an emotion,
according to some psychologists.

Scientific Evidence: Most American adults can
only name three emotions—
happy—sad—angry.

Result: Most American adults
when evaluating a furrowed brow
jump to anger.

Consequence: Confusion.

Summary: This poet is not angry
just puzzled why
you tiptoe by
frightened
of their photo.[1]

---

[1] The first line of this poem was borrowed from 'Unwanted' by Edward Field.

Molly Fisk

Decision Tree

I don't know why, this time, the fire that started six miles away
and grew fast to 50 acres but then was contained would bring
me such flat grief. We didn't even evacuate. I sat on the couch
hearing planes overhead and engines one after another roar
down my street: sirens, red lights, action, retardant, flight plans
reported on Twitter. I couldn't budge myself to gather a thing.

A friend left LA after 30 years to move to Maine, another
is heading for Morro Bay, and now I dream all night of craggy
coastlines and fingers of fog that creep into the folds those hills
make beside the ocean, balsam or live oak dark in the crevices.
I'm getting older, which isn't news, but now I can feel it. Maybe
fear accumulates year after smoky year and we tolerate only

so much of it. Maybe my number is up. I know the sea level's
rising, that storms are fierce, that we'll all die some time.
This fire somehow got under my skin. I think I'd just rather
be drowning than burning.

I Was Slicing a Red Pepper

into salad for dinner and ended up
answering a message about swim times
for tomorrow and then sank into my corner
of the sofa to scroll past the lives of strangers,
really, people I love but have never seen
whole so if I meet them what surprises me
most is their heights. I live in two worlds now:
a house with green leaves out the windows,
pots of purple fountain grass and geraniums
to water every day in summer or believe me
they won't last and then the colors and motion
I hold in my hand, the poems appearing
and vanishing, videos of spoonbills
on the Gulf Coast, racing cheetahs, Humans
of New York, so much life it's impossible
to follow but the flashes of potential fellowship
and happiness, the rueful camaraderie truly
do, in such years of isolation, keep me alive.

Monika Rose

Reunion

A pair of grey doves forage on oat hay seeds
that cows overlooked, not unlike our meal
with fifty years of lost memories while
feeding on a repast of soup

Steam rises from the oily broth
in spicy fragrance, words dance
vessels warm ready hands
where two spoons will work

I scoop regurgitated regret
from a soup of remembering
torn wings bubble and simmer
in a sea of promise

Tongue-tied words curl on the spoon
and then they let go--
like doves at peace
our heads bob
in syllabic descent

Nanci Woody

A Question for the Gods

these weepy eyes
betray the image
of the virile young man
reaching out to you
bouquet of violets in hand
all those decades ago

these brittle bones
now all that's left
for you to cling to
bulging veins on
age-spotted hands
clutch pitifully
this wilting bunch of dandelions

this worn-out body
once vital
vividly remembers
yesterday's
never-ending urge
to touch you
to love you

this overfilled and forgetful brain
lies awake obsessing
about the months
the years spent
needing your hand in mine

this overfilled and hopeful brain
forms a question for the Gods
will I yet be given
a few moments hours days
to hold your hand in mine
to touch you
to love you

Nora Laila Goff

The Poet Shirt

A friend says you have a gift,
you are not using it.
Is a gift a burden? It can be.
It is a responsibility
to care for it, to nurture it
like an heirloom tomato planted in organic soil
to see what multihued unique forms will come
to fruition.
Red, yellow, orange, and green
all in one spherical verse
bursting with juice and fresh from the valley sunshine.

Some readers will scorn your genetically original poems
grown from seeds gathered
from oddly shaped garden tomatoes.
They will buy the GMO,
mealy grocery store flavorless conforming fruit,
all identical off-red ovals picked unripe
spliced with genes that mimic pesticides.
These are the safe supermarket poems people eat up
written by poets with big personalities and fancy pedigrees.

She says you have a gift, do not take it for granted.
Do not fold it neatly and place it in your antique dresser,
take the poet shirt out, put it on, wear it in public,
and don't be afraid of a few ketchup stains.

Oswaldo Vargas

The Son of Something

As penance
for crying to Leona Lewis in the shower
I am the town's newest prodigal son,
marching down the only sidewalk.

I left with deer meat
ground and packaged by my boyhood crush;
he's now a father of four,
for every flannel he left hanging
beside my door.
I come back bearing four stomachs
to stretch them out,
except the breeze's favorite one –
I let it borrow it before I draped the rest
over my home.
Not even a fruit fly can thieve its way in –
only I
can watch who I am.

Patricia Wentzel

Serpent's Bite

> *After Edna St. Vincent Millay following the Uvalde school shooting*

The dirge was sung without music
low, dire, wrenching
for you were all beloved
and we are not reconciled to our loss

We are not reconciled to our loss
your absence a tincture
more potent than the serpent's bite
that strikes down the unsuspecting child

He struck down the unsuspecting children
seeking stardom, fame
left empty halls, scattered books
staring, sunken eyes

Staring, sunken eyes
their hand-hewn caskets delicate
their urns light in their parent's clinging hands
who does not mourn?

Who does not mourn?
who does not fear for the future?
the watchful children left behind?
the teachers who make plans to hide them all?

Who can hide them all?
there is no closet deep enough
no overturned desk, bookcase big enough
no lock strong enough to keep them all safe

No lock can keep them safe
eyes staring, sunken
we shuffle through our days
hearing the echo of gunfire
the cries followed by silence
the dirge sung without music

Paula Sheil

Stone Stone

While I write, the sky sulks,
aftermath of storm
crying over my parched plants,
and I think of desert sands
and women drenched in tears.

It is possible to suffer stoning still.
A two-minute video clip
shows Rokhshana, an Afghan
woman being stoned to death.
She screams with each blow.

Her crime is love; she's an alleged
adulteress, an adulterated
believer in her own pleasure.
Her skin caressed by a boy her age,
not a patriarch.

She cowers in hole, already her grave,
surrounded by men, a mob of stoners
who plea to god for revenge. Her
crime emasculates them. Steals their power.
Her black shroud prevents their gaze.

What does she think as each stone strikes,
turning her flesh into cherry pulp?
Her bones to flaky crust? What does
each stone think as it enters her body?

The men exact their tribute. They
tax her body, redeem her
value unto themselves. Her coin is theirs.
It was never hers. Her light consumable
as fruit and easily digested.

The stones pile up, disappearing her.
Becoming stone only, a monument
to desert sorrow and dessert eaten by men
only. Women. Not.

Still the sky broods. I am here. Cracked.
Not stoned. But broken. The body
knows our darkness, the stoned silence.
The pile of misery.

Randy White

Colonel Liu draws for our Daughter

In the painting life,

one stroke,
is brown like the bend
of the Xiang River, beyond
our house during the rainy season,

in another, a soldier's life,

the enemy advances, fire
is ordered

for the silk factories
to feed on "Dwelling
in the Fuchun Mountains",

on brothers carrying dogwood
up the mountain, until

our countrymen are ash
on *xuan* paper.

One stroke is home, Changsa,
will always be

water on inkstone,
a little sweetness, to the bitter.

Don't ask for food or clothing,
but for a long brush to draw.

In one stroke,

Colonel Liu
draws a leaping cat
for our daughter.

A Vision

Hearing amimi, omiimii, mimia, ori'te, putchee nashoba, jahgowa, meaning big bread. These, being indigenous, should not being strange sounding names for this bird. Sitting there alone it lacks the bluish-gray head and nape, the sides of the neck iridescent feathers bright bronze, violet, golden-green in the angle of this light. Goddess bird once. Wings slate gray tinged with olive brown, that turned into grayish-brown on the lower wings. Where are the thousands millions turning together in the dawn light above an endless forest? Near the wing tip spots random as ink drops. Crying Martha, Martha America lines up in a zoo to see the last Passenger Pigeon now just brown and gray. Her orange-red iris watching us all.

(Short fiction from the novel *The Strange Epic of Homer Vyasa,* one of the eighteen books that constitute *American Mahabharata.*)

Rachael Ikins

The Cat Wears Secret Messages Rolled in Necklace Scrolls: Ars Poetica

~~~~~~~~
Sometimes the tongue scampers off with the mouth, brain not yet on its feet, before words perch like sparrows on the rim of teeth before a subconscious cue, one dark pair of eyes to the next, before the whole flock takes flight. Words swirl through the mind, leave behind one falling feather.
~~~~~~~~~
Excavate the space, wiggle your fingers beneath the web of weed roots. Pull words until your nails grime black, follow the central vine all the way to the seed, cast aside random earth worms, a stone from a cherry, a female spider shriveling around her egg sac. Excavate the darkness, dig until your skin cracks, your nails break. Dig for the melody, the threnody of blackbird voices priming murmuration, heading into the teeth of it.

Rick Rayburn

Sisyphus Symphony

    — north of Trinidad, California

        The clap of cobbles scattered
upslope by rhythmic sea surge—

        like the crack of croquet balls
across Grandpa's green grass—

        drowning out seal barks
every hour, every day,

        year to year.
Rocks tumble

        over the craggy beach,
brattling up,

        clinking down,
surge spraying our forearms,

        shaping stone
into billiard-like balls

        that could clatter
over green felt.

        At sea on my oak mantle
next to Walden Pond quartz,

        two fist-sized round rocks,
greywacke and basalt,

        throttled for 30 years,
still lick of brine.

Sharon Coleman

glow-in-the-dark

```
just blow a hole right through me      mother
adds to her midnight litany        i just want
to die         she wails        gets up to watch
another netflix comedy          i pull a blanket
over my head        soft pink wool from nana
its quality so vintage      flop onto the couch
and let meryl streep's      shapely cheekbones
in a film I saw        some twenty years before
float though               while i half-listen
to the throaty dialogue      fall into the kind
of sleep i'm not sure is sleep      i throw off
the blanket at the film's end           mother's
mind tired          she might manage bed
in a hospital bed she says        other people
have died              in a dark bedroom
her mind won't be distracted       the bedroom
once mine        once painted pink because
i watched too much       i dream of jeannie
walls now lined                 with mom's
landscape paintings          her self-portrait
in the style of chagall's     crowded by nana's
beige armoire and vanity          i once wanted
to paint a glossy dark blue     with gold stars
i've learned            to close the door
on mom's one wish             i cannot fulfill
to her other voice      the wail      the litany
and pull tight the quilt    of the bed she shared
with my father        in the room he died
where she no longer sleeps              tonight
with epic rain i no longer hear         i wait
steaming       for sleep i can know     as sleep
```

salt

grayness cloaks
        her bony shoulders
                soluble
cradled over   a spine bent
in years   too many
she furrows   her hands
                her salt
into a daughter's shoulders
and steady back   bare
except   for willingness

Shawn Pittard

Casting After Shadows

Spring blossoms fall
into their own reflections.

It's been a good year for the dogwood—
a bad year for the homeless.

I surprise a woman washing herself in the river.
We almost say hello.

My mother asked,
Why can't the dead at least come visit?

We were drinking coffee in the kitchen
before first light, before I stepped into the river,

before the sunrise lit the moving waters,
before the horned owl called our names.

Reclamation

For lack of funds, a park
along our urban river
turns wild again.

Blackberries and thorns.
Honey and bees.

Behind a locked gate,
a mountain lion
stalks deer on a dirt trail.
Salmon pulse upstream.

On the bridge above the river,
commuters honk their horns.

Sue Daly

All the Love

When they pass through that portal,
do they ever give us another thought?
Would they send a morsel of affection to
comfort us, after they've gone?

What do they know of us?
What do they care?

Are they so immersed in Heaven's duties,
they cannot spare a moment to remember us?
How could they forget the ones they abandoned,
those who miss them so fiercely?

Do they ever reminisce
about their lives on earth?

And a boy I met at Disneyland the night
before he shipped out to Vietnam, does he
look longingly at me from some low lying cloud,
wishing he had more earth years?

Does he miss all the love
we didn't make?

Susan Flynn
Would You Come If I Called You by Name?

Sister of solitude, Empress of morning,
  hear my clamoring.
    My wanderings await you.

Free me, from my imagining of you.
    Dismember my fantasies.
    Visit me in real time.

As you whisper past my dawn,
     you fill my longing with longing.

In Fall, inside the leaves' dust,
    color moves toward death.

This is my Winter. Make haste.
Leave me not alone another day.

My desire grows dark. My days grow short.
My prayer stumbles toward you.

MARIE

we were a sundial
she at noon, me at six
my feet casting
a shadow between
us

from the light pouring
off her body

she leaned against
her couch's left arm
legs straight out
like in a beach chair

nothing like the beach

her peach silk kimono
sashed at the waist
littered with tiny embroidered
flowers cascading down

such tiny needles, such small hands

exhaustion
also poured off her
alive so many days

past the possible
desirable

I wanted to reach my hand
through the space between us
coax the bird from the sparrow
cage of her body

instead
we sat in silence
drenched with words
from earlier time

quieted now
like a January Christmas tree
ornaments still catching the sun

I bowed
kissed her right hand
resting quiet among silk flowers

in memoriam Marie Reynolds

Taylor Graham

Crystal Water
for Sally

Your husband, snow scientist, is buried.
His death a slow forgetting, the retreat
of glacier. Climate change. You were married
so many years. Remember how we'd meet
to train our dogs – snow burials – a game
for dogs, but serious and scary. Sun
on slope, we learn snow is never the same.
The pure white cornice slides, the snowpacks run.
So many dogs we trained, those years, and lost –
you in snowland, I in a warmer zone.
But everywhere, it seems, we're weather-crossed.
This year, the worst for avalanche we've known.
    I think of you, alone in alpenglow.
    He's gone now to his everlasting snow.

Victoria Dalkey

Sleepwalker

When she walked at night my mother was a searchlight set
off by wind, a raft adrift on shadows.

By day, her eyes asked desperate questions:
To whom should I give the salt and water of

my voice when it boils over, forms a skin
that smells like sorrow? Is this a planet of ice?

If I lick will it pull my tongue out
by the root? Leave me unable to taste but hungry

still? Yet as the moon muscled up
the transom windows on the service porch,

as tall weeds bent in the breeze, she'd whisper
the screen door shut and steer past the palm

(thirsty, yellowing, squat) in front of the abandoned
studio, past the raised bed where

Purple Cherokees, arugula, chard
once grew—now dry dirt and weed

hard as she'd become—no longer the fawn
she was when young, not the daughter tied

to her sister's waist on hot nights when they slept
on the wide veranda. When my mother rose

in sleep, slipped in bare feet down the steps
to walk cool grass, she pulled her sleepy older

sister with her as they entered, merged
with moon-made shadows of trees.

Kulicke's Orange

peeled three quarters down and sitting
      like an offering on a dark
           table in low light. Low light, yet

it glows. You can smell the pungent
      peel, admire its soft white
           pulp, the dome of the translucent

fruit—segments separated by tissue
      that defines the wedges
           to be pulled apart and bitten

so sweetness floods the mouth. Lord
      I now want such an orange!
           But our teak bowl holds only

a pale version that doesn't smell
      at all. My husband cuts it
           and I suck the fruit out

of the rind. The juice is not
      as sweet as I hoped. There is no
           effervescent mist rising

from the peel. No, it can't
      compare to the orange in
           Kulicke's painting.

The orange I deserve.

Thomas Goff

Sistine Lullaby
Michelangelo: Lunette, Hezekiah, Manasseh, Amon

You rest, my baby. You sleep, my child.
One my arms hold, plus one in a cradle,
You who were crying, in my lap I lull you;
You in the low cradle, sleep half a slow dreidel-
Spin and return, just rocking slow.
I love both of you, love to fold you,
You are my clothes, my folds of rose,
Folds of lilac, my soft roll of turban,
Folds of white, of my skin and your skin.
Sleep, my babies, all free from sin.
One of you bundled, lapped in linen,
One of you lain on a padded cradle.
The cradle moves on two smooth curves,
Moves easy and good on curved wood beams,
Made of smooth planks and padded with cloth;
You sway as my foot near your little nose pushes
And you my lap-sleeper, dream and dream
As Moses dreamed in woven rushes.

Shakespeare's Own Columbine

I read a book on tragic Columbine,
The pair of kids who shot up the whole school.
That book, an introduction to the mind-
Set of the active shooter: how as a rule,
We find a "dyadic pair": one psychopath,
One rage-fueled dupe. It certainly happened here.
I read until time to cry, "Hold, enough…"
As I glanced over the demons within, the wrath
In one, the other's coldness without fear
(How can a mere dramatist know of such stuff?),
I shuddered to recognize Iago, the first;
Othello, the second type. One bad, one worst.

Wendy Patrice Williams

Following the Sunlit Trail

Up at the ridgetop
where the basalt rocks grow
up at sky's edge
where juniper juts from stone

I climb, sinking into snow
then wet earth, way above
the homes and ranches and
all the human hopes, cares and dreams

to where bald eagle flies
swooping, scouring the ridgeline
and then, an immature one
wings shining bronze and belly flashing white

flying so low as if to touch rabbit brush,
hush of wind upon us and
sun suddenly doused by a cloud

Time to descend before the snowstorm hits,
go slow, my feet rooted, gravity my friend,
end this sublime journey to basalt cliffs
and snow drifts. Follow the deer tracks back

and then look behind, marvel at how far I've come
from cancer. Smiling now at my luck
and opportunity, let the adventure begin
again and again as I seek the unknown wonder.

Shawn Aveningo-Sanders

Feeding Him Grapes

I remove the white plastic cap from the hospital-supply
        token of comfort
A strong scent of grape
Unexpected pleasure
Among the tubes, the machines, the fear of what's next

His lips so dry
His thirst unquenchable
A simple act
Smearing Chapstick to soothe his cracked mouth
I'm nervous, at first
Which is silly, I know
But I'm afraid of doing anything wrong
Doing anything to bring him even the slightest discomfort
He's been in pain for days now
To take away food
And water
Feels cruel
But necessary to ready him for surgery

We wait
And wait
Try to fill each snail-paced second with distraction
I add another layer of soft grape wax to his lips
He smiles
And laughs a little when I unconsciously open my mouth
In the shape of an O
Mimicking what I need him to do
So I can reach those fragile corners of his mouth
When all I really want to do is kiss him
When all I really want to do is take him home

We repeat this act for hours
He knows how clumsy and helpless I feel
He asks again for a little more Chapstick
Says he can see how much I enjoy helping him
He knows how I need to feel useful

This man of mine
Somehow still wanting to make *me* feel better

That part of his heart—
Not ravaged
Not damaged
His love unwavering
Strong
Like the fruity scent filling our small space of escape
As we perform this act—
Pretending we're in bed
And I'm feeding him grapes

Alexander Antonio Cortez

Mending Petals

Daffodils and dandelions sit:
somber and still, hoping to feel anything but broken.
How much time will pass before they heal?

Tule 89 Review

ABOUT THE CONTRIBUTORS

Lisa Dominguez Abraham's collection *Mata Hari Blows a Kiss* won a Swan Scythe chapbook award, and her book *Coyote Logic* was published by Blue Oak Press. She has recent work in *COMP: an interdisciplinary journal* and *Puerto del Sol*. Newly returned to the San Francisco bay area where she grew up, she now lives in Richmond.

Harrie Alley grew up and fell in love with words in a small Sacramento River Delta town. Her family built a summer cabin in the California foothills. Though she studied at the Iowa City Writers Workshop and traveled far with curiosity, California valleys and foothills remained home. She taught writing and art in valley schools, and recently retired to an oak grove in the foothills, where she lives with family and three hound dogs.

Shawn Aveningo-Sanders is the author of *What She Was Wearing*, an inspirational book of poetry/prose which reveals her #metoo secret — from survival to empowerment. Shawn's work has appeared worldwide in over 160 literary journals and anthologies, including *Calyx, Amsterdam Quarterly, American Journal of Poetry, Timberline Review, Tule Review,* and *Poets Reading the News*, to name a few. She's a Pushcart nominee, Best of the Net nominee, co-founder of The Poetry Box press, and managing editor for *The Poeming Pigeon*. Shawn is a proud mother of three and shares the creative life with her husband, Robert.

Lynn Belzer, a San Francisco native, began her path to poetry in 2016 after losing her husband. Now, retired from her psychotherapy-organizational coaching career, Belzer's work weaves inner and outer life, drawing on nature, art, daily events, and humor. She is active in the Sacramento poetry scene, and has studied with several prominent poets, including Ellen Bass, Susan Kelly-Dewitt, Gillian Conolly and Dorianne Laux.

Doreen Beyer is a recently retired school nurse, a hula dancer, and an emerging poet from Sacramento, California. Her poems have appeared in several anthologies locally and nationally, including *More Than Enough, An Anthology from The Sacramento Poetry Center Writing Groups* (Sacramento Poetry Center, 2023). She is addicted to the written word, her two dogs, red wine and dark chocolate.

Ed Balldinger is a Sacramento native. He once left Sacramento for nine months as an 18 year-old rookie of the road and inexplicably landed in York, Nebraska where he met his soul mate for life. They returned together to Sacramento in 1983 where they raised two sons. He has co-written and performed on 11 albums of music with the WNGC and The Mood Groove. His collection of poetry *From Cavity's Kitchen to the Bone Comber's Home* was published in 2009. He has had poems published in the Cold River Press collections, *Quiet Rooms 2020* and *Voices 2022*. He is currently working on a new collection of poetry.

Julie Hannah Brower is a writer and painter now living in Sacramento, California. She is grateful to be among her family and the trees. She was recently published in *More Than Enough, An Anthology from The Sacramento Poetry Center Writing Groups* (Sacramento Poetry Center, 2023).

Julie Bruck is from Montreal and has lived in San Francisco for over 25 years. Her most recent collection is *How to Avoid Huge Ships* (Brick Books, 2018). Her poems have been widely published, appearing in *Plume, The New Yorker, Poetry Daily, The New Quarterly, The Malahat Review,* and The Academy of American Poets' *Poem-A-Day,* and other venues. Her third book, *Monkey Ranch* (Brick Books), won the 2012 Governor General's Literary Award for poetry. *How to Avoid Huge Ships* was a finalist for the same award in 2019.

John Allen Cann is now an Anchor Bay poet, having moved to the coastal village full-time since stepping away from teaching in Sacramento. His love of the keyboard music of Scarlatti, Schubert & Chopin continues to grow; his passion for well-played baseball has not diminished; his love of laughter and good conversation with friends expands along with the universe. His series "Between – Haiku & Briefings" accompanied an art exhibition, "Thresholds," with painter Mike Connor at Gualala Arts, in October, 2023. His books include *Solitude the Shape of a Woman* (Wooden Angel Press, 1987), *24 Caprices for a Political Year* (Aetheric Press, 1992) and *Moon Over Madrid* (I Street Press, 2016).

Sharon Coleman is a fifth generation Northern Californian with a penchant for languages and their entangled word roots. She has translated poetry from Yiddish, the language of her mother's family, and has studied the Portuguese of her father's. She grew up deeply attuned to seasons, growing cycles — so much of the natural world. Her poetry and prose appear in *Your Impossible Voice, Faultline, The Ana, Dream Pop Press, White Stag, Rivet,* and *Berkeley Poetry Review*. She co-curates the reading series Lyrics & Dirges, at Pegasus Bookstore in Berkeley, and co-directs the Berkeley Poetry Festival. Her books include *Paris Blinks*, micro-fiction (Paper Press, 2016) and *Half Circle*, poetry (Finishing Line Press, 2013). She received the Maverick Award for her poetry from the ruth weiss Foundation (2022), a Luso-American Fellowship for the Disquiet Literary Conference in Lisbon (2018), the Brereton scholarship for the Napa Valley Writers Conference (2021) and was a finalist for the Jane Underwood Poetry Prize (2020).

Linda Jackson Collins has been writing and editing in the Sacramento community for over 10 years. She was an editor of The Sacramento Poetry Center's journal, *Tule Review,* and participates in various writing groups and workshops. Her collection, *Painting Trees,* published by Random Lane Press, won the Gold Medal in poetry from Northern California Publishers and Authors (NCPA) in its 2019 contest. In addition, she has had poetry published in numerous literary journals.

Alexander Antonio Cortez is a 25-year-old performer, writer, mosh pit enthusiast, and tamale lover from Sacramento, California. At open mics, he performs under his childhood nickname, AL. Coming from a Chicano household, his musings range from friends and family, lovers, machismo, yo no sabes, and dreamscapes to self-love and loathing, while also healing his way through mental health, trauma, addiction, and self-love and loathing. His work has appeared in *Fleas on the Dog,* an online literary journal.

Victoria Dalkey is a poet and art critic whose poems have recently appeared in *Birmingham Poetry Review, Bellevue Literary Review* (where she was a finalist for the Marica and Jan Vilcek Poetry Prize), and the anthology *Why From These Rocks: 50 Years of Poems from the Community of Writers* (Heyday Books). She is the author of *twenty.nine.poems* (Redwing Press, 1999), *In the Absence of Silver* (Rattlesnake Press, 2004), and coauthor with Ann Menebroker, Kathryn Hohlwein, and Viola Weinberg Spencer of *Tough Enough: Poems from the Tough Old Broads* (Cold River Press, 2019). She holds a BA and MA in English from California State

University, Sacramento, where she studied with poet Dennis Schmitz. Her art reviews, interviews, and feature stories have appeared in numerous regional and national publications. She is also the author of catalogue essays on contemporary California artists such as Wayne Thiebaud, Manuel Neri, Julia Couzens, and Sheila Sullivan.

Sue Daly's poetry has been featured in several magazines, literary journals, and anthologies. Her chapbook, *A Voice at Last* was published by DAD's DESK Publishing Company in 2017. Her latest book, *Language of the Tea Leaves* was released in May 2021 by Cold River Press.

Lucille Lang Day is the author of seven full-length poetry collections and four chapbooks. Her latest collection is *Birds of San Pancho and Other Poems of Place* (Blue Light Press, 2020). She has also edited the anthology *Poetry and Science: Writing Our Way to Discovery*, coedited *Fire and Rain: Ecopoetry of California* and *Red Indian Road West: Native American Poetry* from California, and published two children's books and a memoir, *Married at Fourteen: A True Story*. Her many honors include the Blue Light Poetry Prize, two PEN Oakland/Josephine Miles Literary Awards, the Joseph Henry Jackson Award, and eleven Pushcart Prize nominations. The founder and publisher of a small press, Scarlet Tanager Books, she lives in Oakland, California.

Karen DeFoe is a performing artist and poet. Her poems have appeared in *Voices of Lincoln Poetry Contest Winners Chapbook* (2019-2022); *Gold Country Writers Poetry Contest Chapbook* (2019-2022); *Ink Spots: Award-winning Flash Fiction and Poetry, Gold Country Writers 10th Anniversary Anthology* (Gold Country Writers Press); and *More Than Enough, An Anthology from The Sacramento Poetry Center Writing Groups* (Sacramento Poetry Center, 2023). She holds a BA in Drama from CSU, San Jose and an MA in Multicultural Education with an emphasis in Gender Equity from CSU, Sacramento.

M. J. Donovan started her writing career coauthoring science textbooks. She has since branched out to more creative endeavors. She currently resides in Sacramento, California among the sycamores and an occasional cacophony of crows. Her poetry has appeared in the *Porter Gulch Review* and *Catamaran Literary Reader*.

Molly Fisk edited *California Fire & Water, A Climate Crisis Anthology*, with a Poets Laureate Fellowship from the Academy of American Poets. She's the author of *The More Difficult Beauty, Listening to Winter,* and *Everything But the Kitchen Skunk,* among other books, and has won grants from the NEA, the California Arts Council, and the Corporation for Public Broadcasting. Fisk lives in the Sierra foothills, where she provides weekly commentary to community radio, and works as a radical life coach.

Susan Flynn is a poet, photographer and psychologist living in Sacramento and Georgetown, California. Her first poetry collection, *Seeing Begins in the Dark*, was published by River Rock Books of Sacramento in June 2022. Susan facilitates writing groups for trauma survivors, and in her capacity as Assistant Clinical Professor in the UC Davis Psychiatry Department she is involved with Narrative Psychiatry utilizing writing and literature as part of clinical treatment.

Catherine French was born and grew up in Sacramento, and teaches in the community college system. She earned an MFA at U Arizona and won the James D. Phelan Award from the San Francisco Foundation for manuscript in progress. This manuscript became the book *Sideshow*, published by University of Nevada Press in 2002. Her work has appeared in *The Nation, The Gettysburg Review, The Iowa Review*, and other journals.

Diane Funston lives in Marysville, California. She has been published in various journals including *California Quarterly, Synkronicity, San Diego Poetry Annual, Whirlwind, Summation,* and *Palettes and Quills*, among others. She has been the Poet-in-Residence for Yuba-Sutter Arts and Culture for two years and ran a monthly Zoom event called "Poetry Square" featuring poets from all over. Her first chapbook, *Over The Falls*, is newly out from Foothills Publishing.

Laura Garfinkel is a retired social worker who worked mostly in geriatrics and spent years trying to learn from her clients to imagine life at the end, looking back. Now that she is getting older herself, she is trying to live fully, looking forward. Still, she spends much of her time reflecting and putting words, images, and memories down on the page like any devoted poet who tries to capture life in words. Her work has been published in *Poetica* and *Salt Water*.

Nora Laila Goff is a poet and watercolor artist who paints landscapes and flower close-ups and has shown her work at the Sacramento Fine Arts Center. Her chapbook of poetry is called *The River Speaks* (Poet's Corner Press). She has been published in *The American River Review, Poetry Now, One Dog Press, The Zangspur Review* and elsewhere.

Thomas Goff is an instructional assistant in Folsom Lake College's Reading and Writing Center, and a frequent performer on trumpet with Golden State Brass, Auburn Symphony, and Camellia Symphony. His poem "Blind Tom's 'Battle of Manassas'" won the Robinson Jeffers Tor House Prize for Poetry in 2021. His poems have been published most recently in *Spectral Realms* (Hippocampus Press) and FLC's *The Parlay*, and he is represented in *Fire and Rain: Ecopoetry of California* (2018). Tom's work as a reviewer has appeared in *Poetry Flash*, and a review of Brad Buchanan's *Chimera* appeared in the February 2023 issue of SPC'S Poet News.

Connie Gutowsky is a retired defense attorney. Her poems and essays have appeared in literary journals, travel books and two chapbooks. Recently widowed, she now resides at Oakmont of East Sacramento and spends time with her two beloved sons and four grandchildren. Her book *PLAY* was published by Random Lane Press. Her illustration graces the cover of this issue of *Tule Review*.

Taylor Graham is a volunteer search-and-rescue dog handler and served as El Dorado County's first Poet Laureate (2016-18). Her work is included in the anthologies *California Poetry: From the Gold Rush to the Present, California Fire & Water: A Climate Crisis Anthology,* and *Villanelles* (Everyman's Library). Her latest books are *Uplift* (2016) and *Windows of Time and Place* (2019), both from Cold River Press.

Dianna Henning taught classes through California Poets in the Schools, and poetry workshops through the William James Association's Prison Arts Program, including Folsom Prison. She received several California Arts Council grants, and has run The

Thompson Peak Writers' Workshop in Lassen County for the last twenty-eight years. Her work has been published in *Worth More Standing, Poets and Activists Pay Homage to Trees, Voices, MacQueen's Quinterly, Artemis Journal, 2021 & 2022; The Adirondack Review, Memoir Magazine, The Plague Papers, Pacific Poetry*, and *New American Writing*. She was nominated for a Pushcart Prize in 2021 by The Adirondack Review. Her fourth collection of poetry *Camaraderie of the Marvelous* was published by Kelsay Books in September 2021. She has an MFA in Writing from Vermont College, Montpelier, VT.

Jan Haag taught writing as a journalism/creative writing professor in Sacramento, California, for more than three decades. Now retired, she hosts writing workshops using the Amherst Writers & Artists method. She is the author of a poetry collection, *Companion Spirit*, (Amherst Writers & Artists Press) and has had stories and poems published in many anthologies and literary journals.

Rachael Ikins is a 2016/18 Pushcart and 2013/18 CNY Book Award nominee, a 2018 Independent Book Award winner, a 2019 Vinnie Ream & Faulkner poetry finalist, and a 2021 Best of the Net nominee. She is the author/illustrator of nine books in multiple genres. Her writing and artwork have appeared in journals worldwide from India, the UK, Japan, Canada and the US. Born in the Finger Lakes, she lives by a river with her dogs, cats, saltwater fish, a garden that feeds her through winter and riotous houseplants with a room of their own. She is a graduate of Syracuse University, and Associate Editor of Clare Songbirds Publishing House.

Anthony Xavier Jackson is a poet and musician whose work may be found on SoundCloud and Bandcamp. Jackson has been writing since his teenaged years. Surreal, complex, musical imagery, magician ramblings, autobiographical musings describe his work. From The Last Poets to Nikki Giovanni, from Punk Rock to Crossroads Blues, Anthony is a proud inheritor of the traditions of Afropunk, Afrosurrealism, Afrofuturism — all wrapped up in a 21st century American experience.

Andy Jones is Poet Laureate *emeritus* of Davis, California. He has taught writing, creative writing, and literature classes at the University of California, Davis since 1990, and has hosted the fortnightly Poetry Night Reading Series in Davis since 2007. His books of poetry include *Split Stock, Where's Jukie?,* and *In the Almond Orchard: Coming Home from War*. His work has also appeared in small journals and magazines, and anthologies such as *Flatman Crooked's Slim Anthology of Contemporary Poetics*.

Laura King holds a Master of Divinity degree from Union Theological Seminary in New York City. Her work has appeared in *Neologism Journal, The Opiate Magazine, Modern Haiku, Ponder Review, Evening Street Review, Wrath Bearing Tree, Hollins Critic, whimperbang, Slant, The Meadow, FRiGG, Visitant, El Portal, Dash, Phoenix* and *The Los Angeles Times*. She lives in Sacramento, California, where she is a hospital chaplain.

Mary Mackey is the author of eight collections of poetry including *Sugar Zone*, which won the 2012 PEN Oakland/Josephine Miles Award; and *The Jaguars That Prowl Our Dreams*, which won both the 2019 Eric Hoffer Small Press Award for the best book published by a small press and a 2018 CIIS Women's Spirituality Book Award. Her poems have been praised by Wendell Berry, Jane Hirshfield, D. Nurkse, Al Young, Maxine Hong Kingston, Dennis Schmitz, and Marge Piercy for their beauty, precision, originality, and extraordinary range. She is also a New York Times bestselling author of 14 novels.

Mary McGrath, storyteller and poet, spent many years producing storytelling and poetry programs in Sacramento. In addition to her own work, she performed works from Irish Mythology with harpist Alex Ives. She wrote the syllabus for a course in storytelling at Sacramento City College, and taught the art of storytelling in schools, libraries and museums. She was the author of *The Farmer, the Thief and the Pumpkin Patch*. She was a Peig Sayers Scholar, and won the 2019 Oracle Award from the National Storytelling Network, honoring her four decades of distinguished and passionate work. Through her work, she brought relief to abused women, entertainment to classroom-weary youngsters, and self-esteem and confidence to adults yearning to perfect their oratorical skills. She earned her Master's degree in early childhood education from Sacramento State. Mary McGrath passed away in April 2023.

Thomas Mitchell was raised in New York and California but has lived in Oregon since 1980. He received his MA from California State University, Sacramento, where he studied with the poet Dennis Schmitz. He received an MFA from the University of Montana, where he worked with Richard Hugo and Madeline De Frees. His first collection of poems, *The Way Summer Ends*, was published in 2016, followed by *Caribou* in 2018. *Where We Arrive*, published by Lost Horse Press, is his most recent book. Mitchell's poems have appeared in many journals, including *The New England Review, New Letters, Miramar Magazine,* and *Valparaiso Poetry Review*.

J. C. (Chris) Olander has been a bio-educator with California Poets in the Schools since 1984, and is an innovator of spoken word poetry arising from land-based ethics rooted in science, observation, and reflection. He explores human horrors and beautiful auras of mystical revelations and all that is possible in being here now. He writes, "What we make of life is what we get. I create musical image phrasing to dramatize relative experiences; a sound poet exploring meanings of words, phrases, ideas, and emotions in sound rhythm patterns." He teaches poetry writing and recitation in California schools, and has four spoken word CDs, and four of poetry with musicians. His poetry collections include *River Light* (Poetic Matrix Press), and *Twilight Roses* (R. L. Crow Press).

Jennifer O'Neill Pickering is a literary and visual artist. Her short stories and poetry are published in print, audio and online. She's a Pushcart Nominee for Poetry and a finalist in the New Women's Voices Chapbook Competition. Her poem "I Am the Creek" was selected for the site-specific sculpture, Open Circle. *Fruit Box Castles: Poems from a Peach Rancher's Daughter* was published by Finishing Line Press.

Shawn Pittard is the author of two slender volumes of poetry: *Standing in the River*, which was the winner of Tebot Bach's 2010 Clockwise Chapbook Competition, and *These Rivers*, published by Rattlesnake Press.

Danyen Powell is currently the facilitator for the Sacramento Poetry Center's weekly Tuesday Night Workshop. His work has been published in *Brevities, Pudding Magazine, The Poets' Guild, Poetry Depth Quarterly, Chrysanthemum, Rattlesnake Review, The Sacramento Anthology: One Hundred Poems* and elsewhere. His chapbooks include *Anvil* (Rattle Snake Press, 2004) and *Blue Sky Flies Out*

(Rattlesnake Press, 2008). *Words Die Of Thirst*, poems in English translated into Spanish by Roberto Knorr, was published in 2014.

Gordon Preston attended San Diego State where he began his poetry writing endeavors. He has written six chapbooks and has been published with great gratitude by small presses and literary journals. Finishing Line Press published his first chapbook, *Violins*. He has had poems published in *Blue Mesa Review, Comstock Review, Cutbank, The Missouri Review, Rattle, Tar Wolf Review*, and others. He has lived in Modesto for a long time and was a founding member of the Modesto-Stanislaus Poetry Center (MoSt).

Ann Privateer is a poet, artist, and photographer. She grew up in the Midwest and now resides in California. Some of her recent work has appeared in *Voices 2018* and *2022, Third Wednesday,* and *Carolina Muse* among other places.

Melinda Moore Rivasplata holds a BA degree in Environmental Biology from the University of California at Santa Barbara. Her career has included work in environmental education, resource management with the US Forest Service, and environmental planning and regulation compliance. Her poems have been published in the anthology *Late Peaches* in 2012 and in *Poems By Sacramento Poets, Cosumnes River Journal* in 2017.

Rick Rayburn has resided in Altadena (a 4th generation Angeleno), Arcata on Humboldt Bay, and Sacramento. He began work at the Coastal Commission as a redwood ecologist, then a land preservationist at California State Parks. Retired, he moved from environmental protection to writing, beginning with an eco-poetry class in 2015. His book, *Under the Overstory*, was published by Random Lane Press in 2020. Random Lane released his second book, *Slack Tide*, in May 2023.

Monika Rose lives in the foothills of Calaveras County, and is founding director and editor of Manzanita Writers Press, a nonprofit literary publisher. She has been published in several anthologies and literary magazines. Her book of poems, *River by the Glass*, by GlenHill Publishing, and *Bed Bumps*, a children's book, will soon be joined by a novel, a collection of short fiction, a second children's book, and a new poetry collection. She has edited numerous Manzanita anthologies, including *Out of the Fire, Wild Edges, Pieces, Wine, Cheese & Chocolate,* and *Voices of Wisdom*, plus several Manzanita prose and poetry anthologies, as well as novels, poetry, and nonfiction for many regional authors. She is Adjunct Associate Professor of English at San Joaquin Delta College, as well as a workshop leader for many regional writers conferences and writing classes.

Jonathan (Jack) Schouten lives in Sacramento with his wife and their three dogs. He has two lovely daughters, Griffin and Tallulah. He received his MA in Poetry at CSUS where he studied under Dennis Schmitz. He currently teaches at Solano Community College.

Bob Stanley studied poetry at UCLA with Stephen Yenser, and taught English and Creative Writing at Sacramento City College and CSU, Sacramento, before retiring in 2021. President of Sacramento Poetry Center for 12 years, Bob organized hundreds of poetry events, and served as Poet Laureate of Sacramento City and County from 2009 to 2012. He edited two anthologies of California poets, *Late Peaches* (2013), and *Sometimes in the Open* (2009). His own books include *Walt Whitman Orders a Cheeseburger* (Rattlesnake Press, 2009), and *Miracle Shine* (CW

Books, 2013). Bob lives in Sacramento with his wife, Joyce Hsiao, where they run online poetry seminars to help support local nonprofits, and operate Random Lane Press. His book *Language Barrier* is forthcoming from CW Books in 2024.

Jamie Seibel earned a Master's Degree in English with a concentration in Creative Writing from California State University, Sacramento. Her work is forthcoming in *Versification Poetry Zine, Wingless Dreamer, The Chamber Magazine, The Tiger Moth Review, Plum Tree Tavern,* and *Poetry Pacific*. Her poem "Children of the Sea" was a top finalist for Wingless Dreamer's Seashore Contest. Overall, Jamie's work focuses on mortality, transformation, and the environment.

Paula Sheil is a published poet and award-winning journalist. She teaches writing and poetry at San Joaquin Delta College and is the founder of Tuleburg Press, a nonprofit publishing company, and The Write Place, a creative writing and book arts center, both in Stockton, CA.

Jill Stockinger obtained her MLS from the University of Wisconsin-Madison, served as a librarian in large library systems for 42 years and ran an open writing group for 16 years. Her poems have been published in small literary magazines, including *Did We Not Meet, Spectrum, Voices 2021* and *Primavera*. Retired, she writes daily. She also spends more time than she should playing online games.

Linda Toren is a retired teacher and currently director of Voices of Wisdom through Manzanita Writer's Press (MWP). She has presented poetry workshops for children and adults — publishing school-wide collections of poetry and art at local elementary schools for more than 20 years. She is currently Poet Laureate of Calaveras County (2022-2024). She produces a community radio program at KQBM Blue Mountain which streams live at KQBM.org the 2nd and 4th Wednesdays from 3:00 to 4:30 p.m. Archived shows can be found at lindatoren.com (click on the radio). It's a program dedicated to poetry, prose, nonfiction literary news, lyrics, and the celebration of thoughts and language.

Georgette Unis is the author of two books of poetry, *Watercolors in the Desk Drawer* (2022) and *Tremors* (2018) published by Finishing Line Press. Her poems have appeared in several literary journals, among them *Naugatuck River Review, San Pedro River Review, Southwestern American Literature* and *Ginosko Literary Review*. She leads the Gold Country Writers poetry workshop and is a member of the Ravens poetry group. She has an MFA in mixed media painting and has exhibited her artwork in many solo and group exhibitions. She maintains her home and studio in the Sierra foothills of northern California where she lives with her husband of fifty-two years.

Oswaldo Vargas is a former farmworker, a graduate of the University of California, Davis and a 2021 recipient of the Undocupoets Fellowship. His work is included in the anthologies *Nepantla: An Anthology Dedicated to Queer Poets of Color, Puro Chicanx Writers of the 21st Century,* and *Imaniman: Poets Writing in the Anzaldúan Borderlands*. He has also been published in *Narrative, Queen Mob's Teahouse, Huizache* and *The Louisville Review*. He lives and dreams in Sacramento, California.

Gillian Wegener is the author of *The Opposite of Clairvoyance* (2008) and *This Sweet Haphazard* (2017), poetry collections published by Sixteen Rivers Press. She's a former Poet Laureate for the City of Modesto and the co-founder and president of the Modesto-Stanislaus Poetry Center, a nonprofit promoting poetry throughout Stanislaus County.

David Weinshilboum grew up in Minnesota, and because of the state's linguistic eccentricities, for years believed that the children's tag game was universally known as "Duck, Duck, Gray-duck." He is an English professor at Cosumnes River College and lives in Davis with his wife, Megan. He studied non-fiction with Elmaz Abinader at Mills College from 1995 to 1997, and honed his writing skills as a journalist for regional publications including the Davis Enterprise, the Sacramento Business Journal and UC Davis Magazine. Since 2003, he has been an English professor at Cosumnes River College. His creative work has been published in *The Walrus* and *The Suisun Valley Review*.

Patricia Wentzel has been writing poetry for about eight years as part of her recovery from a Bipolar Disorder episode. She and her family live in Sacramento, CA. Her calico cat Margie helped her write this bio. She has been published in the *Journal of the American Medical Association, The Light Ekphrastic, Poetry Now, Muse, The Voices Project* and others. Her life as a poet has been nurtured by the Women's Wisdom Art program, the Sacramento Prose and Poetry Meetup, and Sacramento Poetry Center members.

Randy White is the author of *Blood Transparencies* and *Motherlode/La Veta Madre*, two of the eighteen books that comprise the epic poem "American Mahabharata." His work has appeared in numerous magazines including *Sulfur, The Notre Dame Review*, and *News of Native California*. In 2016 he was nominated for a Pulitzer Prize in Autobiography. In Rocklin, California he manages the Blue Oak Press which recently published *They Rise Like a Wave: An Anthology of Asian American Women Poets*.

Wendy Patrice Williams is the author of *In Chaparral: Life on the Georgetown Divide, California* (Cold River Press), a collection of poems, and two chapbooks. Her memoir *Autobiography of a Sea Creature: Healing the Trauma of Infant Surgery* will be published in the summer of 2023 by University of California Health Humanities Press.

Nanci Lee Woody was a college professor, textbook author and Dean of Business before writing her first novel *Tears and Trombones* which won an Independent Publishers award for "Best Fiction in the Western Pacific Region," as well as other awards. She has published many short stories and poems in print anthologies and online magazines. She just completed the pilot to convert *Tears and Trombones* to an eight-episode streaming series.

George Yatchisin is Communications Director for the Gevirtz Graduate School of Education at UC Santa Barbara, and author of the chapbook *Feast Days* (Flutter Press 2016), and the full length collection *The First Night We Thought the World Would End* (Brandenburg Press 2019). His poems have been published in journals including *Antioch Review, Askew,* and *Zocalo Public Square,* and in the anthologies *Reel Verse: Poems About the Movies* (Everyman's Library 2019), *Clash by Night* (City Lit Press 2015), *and Buzz* (Gunpowder Press 2014). He is co-editor of the anthology *Rare Feathers: Poems on Birds & Art* (Gunpowder Press 2015).

Chryss Yost is a poet, designer, and educator based in Santa Barbara, California. She is the co-editor of Gunpowder Press, an independent poetry publisher, and principal of Sungold Editions. She served as Santa Barbara Poet Laureate from 2013-2015. She was awarded the Patricia Dobler Poetry Prize from Carlow University (selected by Patricia Smith) and has been nominated for the Pushcart Prize. Her collection, *Ornamented* was published by The Night Heron Barks, in Spring 2021.

Andrena Zawinski's poems have received accolades for lyricism, spirituality, social concern and have appeared in *Blue Collar Review, Artemis Journal, Rattle, Progressive Magazine*, and others with work online at *Women's Voices for Change, Writing in a Woman's Voice, Verse Daily* and elsewhere. Her fourth full-length collection of poetry is *Born Under the Influence* (WordTech, 2022).

ABOUT THE EDITOR

Susan Kelly-DeWitt is a former Wallace Stegner Fellow and the author of *Gatherer's Alphabet* (Gunpowder Press, CA Poets Prize, 2022), *Gravitational Tug* (Main Street Rag, 2020), *Spider Season* (Cold River Press, 2016), *The Fortunate Islands* (Marick Press, 2008) and a number of previous small press collections. Her work has also appeared in many anthologies, and in print and online journals at home and abroad. She is currently a member of the National Book Critics Circle, the Northern California Book Reviewers Association and a contributing editor for Poetry Flash. For more information, please visit her website at www.susankelly-dewitt.com.

Tule 100 Review

Made in the USA
Middletown, DE
22 March 2024